MW01202188

FREE DVD FREE DVD

Essential Test Tips DVD from Trivium Test Prep

Dear Customer,

Thank you for purchasing from Cirrus Test Prep! Whether you're looking to join the military, get into college, or advance your career, we're honored to be a part of your journey.

To show our appreciation (and to help you relieve a little of that test-prep stress), we're offering a **FREE** *Praxis Essential Test Tips DVD** by Cirrus Test Prep. Our DVD includes 35 test preparation strategies that will help keep you calm and collected before and during your big exam. All we ask is that you email us your feedback and describe your experience with our product. Amazing, awful, or just so-so: we want to hear what you have to say!

To receive your **FREE** *Praxis Essential Test Tips DVD*, please email us at 5star@ cirrustestprep.com. Include "Free 5 Star" in the subject line and the following information in your email:

1. The title of the product you purchased.
2. Your rating from 1 – 5 (with 5 being the best).
3. Your feedback about the product, including how our materials helped you meet your goals and ways in which we can improve our products.
4. Your full name and shipping address so we can send your **FREE** *Praxis Essential Test Tips DVD*.

If you have any questions or concerns please feel free to contact us directly at 5star@cirrustestprep.com.

Thank you, and good luck with your studies!

* Please note that the free DVD is <u>not included</u> with this book. To receive the free DVD, please follow the instructions above.

Praxis II World and US History Content Knowledge (5941) Rapid Review Study Guide:

Comprehensive Review with Practice Test Questions

J.G. Cox

Copyright ©2021 by Cirrus Test Prep

ISBN-13: 9781637981252

ALL RIGHTS RESERVED. By purchase of this book, you have been licensed one copy for personal use only. No part of this work may be reproduced, redistributed, or used in any form or by any means without prior written permission of the publisher and copyright owner. Cirrus Test Prep; Trivium Test Prep; Accepted, Inc.; and Ascencia Test Prep are all imprints of Trivium Test Prep, LLC.

Cirrus Test Prep is not affiliated with or endorsed by any testing organization and does not own or claim ownership of any trademarks, specifically for the Praxis World and US History: Content Knowledge (0941/5941) exam. All test names (and their acronyms) are trademarks of their respective owners. This study guide is for general information only and does not claim endorsement by any third party.

Image(s) used under license from Shutterstock.com

About the Author

Caroline Brennan spent several years on the front lines of multilateral diplomacy at the United Nations, working with the International Committee of the Red Cross (ICRC) in humanitarian affairs from 2007 – 2012. Previously, she studied international development, postcolonial theory, and history in Canada, Europe, and North Africa; she obtained her master's degree from the University of Pennsylvania in 2007, specializing in Middle Eastern history.

Table of Contents

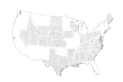

Online Resources

To help you fully prepare for your Praxis World and US History (5941) exam, Cirrus includes online resources with the purchase of this study guide.

PRACTICE TEST

In addition to the practice test included in this book, we also offer an online exam. Since many exams today are computer based, getting to practice your test-taking skills on the computer is a great way to prepare.

FLASH CARDS

A convenient supplement to this study guide, Cirrus's flash cards enable you to review important terms easily on your computer or smartphone.

CHEAT SHEETS

Review the core skills you need to master the exam with easy-to-read Cheat Sheets.

FROM STRESS TO SUCCESS

Watch From Stress to Success, a brief but insightful YouTube video that offers the tips, tricks, and secrets experts use to score higher on the exam.

REVIEWS

Leave a review, send us helpful feedback, or sign up for Cirrus promotions—including free books!

Access these materials at:

www.cirrustestprep.com/praxis-5941-online-resources

Introduction

Congratulations on choosing to take the Praxis World and US History: Content Knowledge (0941/5941) exam! By purchasing this book, you've taken the first step toward becoming a history teacher.

This guide will provide you with a detailed overview of the Praxis, so you know exactly what to expect on test day. We'll take you through all the concepts covered on the test and give you the opportunity to test your knowledge with practice questions. Even if it's been a while since you last took a major test, don't worry; we'll make sure you're more than ready!

WHAT IS THE PRAXIS?

Praxis Series tests are a part of teaching licensure in approximately forty states. Each state uses the tests and scores in different ways, so be sure to check the certification requirements in your state by going to www.ets.org/Praxis/states. There, you will find information detailing the role of the Praxis tests in determining teaching certification in your state, what scores are required, and how to transfer Praxis scores from one state to another. The assessment will measure your aptitude in history and prepare you for a career in teaching world and US history courses.

WHAT'S ON THE PRAXIS?

The content in this guide will prepare you for the Praxis World and US History: Content Knowledge (0941/5941) exam. The test with code 0941 is a pencil-and-paper test, while the test with code 5941 is a computer-administered test. Both are a multiple-choice tests that assess whether you possess the knowledge and skills necessary to become a history teacher. You have a maximum of two hours to complete the 120-question test.

Praxis World and US History: Content Knowledge (0941/5941) Content		
Concepts	Approximate Number of Questions per Subject	Percentage of Test
World History to 1450 C.E.	30	25%
World History: 1450 C.E. to the present	30	25%
United States History to 1877	30	25%
United States History 1877 to the present	30	25%
Total	**120**	**100% (2 hours)**

The Praxis is comprised primarily of questions intended to test your knowledge of historical facts. Other questions on the Praxis also gauge historical thinking skills. Thinking historically entails constructing historical questions, assessing primary and secondary sources, formulating historical arguments, drawing connections, evaluating causation of historical events, and putting events in a global and historical context. Some of these questions may ask you to interpret maps, cartoons, texts, and/or graphs. Historical thinking skills questions are dispersed throughout the test and subject areas and encompass approximately 25 percent of the test.

You will answer approximately sixty multiple-choice questions (50 percent of the test) on United States history. The test will require knowledge of North American geography, pre-colonial civilizations, the purposes of European colonization of the continent, and how pre-colonial peoples interacted with European colonizers. Be prepared for questions about the American Revolution and the foundations of the United States government and Constitution. The test will cover developments in the nineteenth century, including westward expansion, political division, the Civil War, Reconstruction, industrialization, urbanization, and immigration. The Progressive Era and the New Deal are covered as well. Be aware not only of United States involvement in the First and Second World Wars, but also of their impact on both foreign and domestic policy. Prepare for thematic questions that will test your knowledge of the impact of labor and technology on the economy, changing political trends from the New Deal and Great Society to conservatism, the impact of religion on society, and civil rights and changing perceptions of race, ethnicity and gender roles throughout the twentieth century. Questions are also likely to explore the United States' role as a world power during the Cold War and into the twenty-first century.

You will answer approximately sixty multiple-choice questions (50 percent of the test) on world history. In general, you will be expected to understand how world societies and civilizations have been shaped by conflict, technology, and religion; ideologies like nationalism, totalitarianism, and other political philosophies; economic movements like industrialization and the market economy; and major demographic trends. The test will also presume an understanding of transglobal similarities in gender and family expectations, and the impact of trade within and between cultures. Specific questions may ask about the classical civilizations in Europe and Asia and their transformation from 300 – 1400 C.E.; European developments from the Renaissance through the Enlightenment; colonization, trade, and other global interactions from 1200 – 1750 C.E.; the consequences of nationalism and European imperialism from 1750 – 1914 C.E.; the causes and consequences of the First and Second World Wars (like decolonization and the rise of the Soviet Union); and the important developments of the post-Cold War world (such as globalization and fundamentalism).

How is the Praxis Scored?

Your scores become available two to three weeks after the exam on your online account; you will be notified via email when they are released. When you register, you may choose four recipient institutions for your scores; they will be sent directly for free. After your scores become available, you may send them to other institutions for an additional charge. Some states are automatic score recipients. Check www.ets.org to determine how this applies to your specific situation.

Each multiple-choice question is worth one raw point. The total number of questions you get correct is added up to obtain your raw score, which is then scaled to result in your final score. Keep in mind that some multiple-choice questions are experimental questions for the purpose of the Praxis test-makers and will not count toward your overall score. However, since those questions are not indicated on the test, you must respond to every question. There is no penalty for guessing on Praxis tests, so be sure to eliminate answer choices and answer every question. If you still do not know the answer, guess; you may get it right!

How is the Praxis Administered?

The Praxis World and US History test with code 0941 is a pencil-and-paper test, while the test with code 5941 is a computer administered test. You are encouraged to take the version of the test that is most comfortable for you. There is no difference between the two versions; both have the same time-limit and cover the same content. The Praxis website allows you to take a practice test to acclimate yourself to the computerized format.

The Praxis Series tests are available at testing centers across the nation. To find a testing center near you, go to http://www.ets.org/Praxis/register. At this site, you can create a Praxis account, check testing dates, register for a test, or find instructions for registering via mail or phone.

On the day of your test, be sure to bring your admission ticket (which is provided when you register) and photo ID. The testing facility will provide pencils and erasers and an area outside of the testing room to store your personal belongings. You are allowed no personal effects in the testing area. Cell phones and other electronic, photographic, recording, or listening devices are not permitted in the testing center at all, and bringing those items may be cause for dismissal, forfeiture of your testing fees, and cancellation of your scores. For details on what is and is not permitted at your testing center, refer to http://www.ets.org/Praxis/test_day/bring.

About Cirrus Test Prep

Cirrus Test Prep study guides are designed by current and former educators and are tailored to meet your needs as an incoming educator. Our guides offer all of the resources necessary to help you pass teacher certification tests across the nation.

Cirrus clouds are graceful, wispy clouds characterized by their high altitude. Just like cirrus clouds, Cirrus Test Prep's goal is to help educators "aim high" when it comes to obtaining their teacher certification and entering the classroom.

How to Use This Guide

This guide will help you master the most important test topics and also develop critical test-taking skills. We have built features into our books to prepare you for your tests and increase your score. Along with a detailed summary of the test's format, content, and scoring, we offer an in-depth overview of the content knowledge required to pass the test. Our sidebars provide interesting information, highlight key concepts, and review content so that you can solidify your understanding of the exam's concepts. Test your knowledge with sample questions and detailed answer explanations in the text that help you think through the problems on the exam and two full-length practice tests that reflect the content and format of the Praxis. We're pleased you've chosen Cirrus to be a part of your professional journey.

World History

EARLY CIVILIZATIONS AND THE GREAT EMPIRES

PALEOLITHIC AND NEOLITHIC ERAS

The earliest humans were hunter-gatherers until the development of agriculture in about 11,000 BCE. 60,000–70,000 years ago, early humans began migrating from Africa, gradually spreading out across the continents.

Early human history begins with the **Paleolithic** era. During this period, early **hominids** like our ancestors *Homo sapiens sapiens* and *Homo neanderthalensis* exhibited the use of rudimentary tools based on stone, before metalworking. Hence, the term *Stone Age* describes this period.

From approximately 11,000–10,500 BCE, humans started settled communities, developed agricultural practices, and began domesticating animals. They also started using metal to make tools, weapons, and other objects. This was the beginning of the **Neolithic** period, characterized by behavioral and technological change like the invention of the wheel. During the **Bronze Age**, humans began working with copper and tin, creating stronger tools and weapons.

MIDDLE EAST AND EGYPT

Settled societies organized into larger centralized communities characterized by early social stratification and rule of law. The earliest known examples of these were in the **Fertile Crescent**, the area in North Africa and Southwest Asia stretching from Egypt through the Levant and into Mesopotamia.

Around 2500 BCE the **Sumerians** emerged in the Near East. Developing irrigation and advanced agriculture, they were able to develop city-states. They also invented **cuneiform**, the first alphabet, which allowed advanced governance and administration. Sumer featured city-states, the potter's wheel, early astronomy and mathematics, literature, and religious thought.

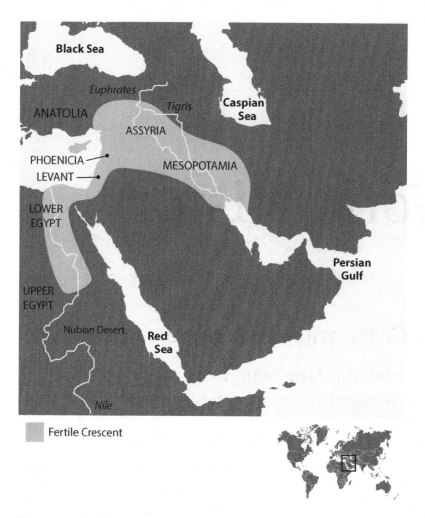

Figure 2.1. Fertile Crescent

Eventually the Sumerians were overcome by Semitic-speaking, nomadic peoples in the Fertile Crescent: the result was the **Akkadian Empire**. Around the eighteenth century BCE, the Akkadians had given way to **Babylonia** in Southern Mesopotamia and **Assyria** in the north. These two civilizations would develop roughly concurrently.

Assyria had developed as a powerful city-state in northern Mesopotamia. Influenced by the Sumerians and Akkadians, the Assyrians developed unique sculpture and jewelry, established regional military dominance, and played an important role in regional trade. At odds with Babylonia over the centuries, the Assyrian Empire had grown to encompass most of the Fertile Crescent.

Like Assyria, Babylonia inherited elements of Akkadian and Sumerian civilization. By the eighteenth century BCE, King Hammurabi in Babylonia had developed courts and an early codified rule of law—**the Code of Hammurabi**—which meted out justice on an equal basis: "an eye for an eye, a tooth for a tooth."

Babylonia continued urban development supported by organized agriculture, warfare, administration, and justice; Babylon became a major ancient city. Babylonia developed more advanced astronomy, medicine, mathematics, philosophy, art, and literature like the *Epic of Gilgamesh*.

Around 1200 BCE Mesopotamia became vulnerable to the **Hittites** from Anatolia. The Hittites had developed in the Bronze Age but flourished in the **Iron Age**, developing expertise in metallurgy to create strong weapons; they also mastered horsemanship and invented chariots. Thus the Hittites became a strong military power and a threat to regional empires and their commercial interests.

> **DID YOU KNOW?**
>
> Settled communities needed the reliable sources of food and fresh water a temperate climate could provide. Surpluses of food allowed for cultural and civilizational development, not just survival.

Meanwhile, development had been under way in the **Nile Valley** in ancient **Egypt**. Known for their pyramids, art, and pictorial writing (**hieroglyphs**), the ancient Egyptians emerged as early as 5000 BCE; evidence of Egyptian unity under one monarch, or **pharaoh**, dates to the First Dynasty, around 3000 BCE.

Despite the surrounding Sahara Desert, the land along the Nile River was arable. Irrigation enabled the Egyptians to develop settled communities. Civilizations emerged on the Upper and Lower Nile, unifying under the early dynasties led by pharaohs, with the Egyptian capital at **Memphis**.

By the fourth dynasty, Egypt's civilizational institutions, written language, art, and architecture were well developed. It was during this period that the famous **pyramids** were erected at Giza as burial tombs. In addition, the complex religious mythology of ancient Egypt had become established. Egypt grew in power from 1550 to 1290 BCE. Led by the powerful Pharaoh **Thutmose III**, Egypt expanded into the Levant.

Later, **King Akhenaten (Amenhotep IV)** abolished the Egyptian religion, establishing a cult of the sun linked to himself. During this period Egypt saw a surge of iconoclastic art and sculpture. However, his successors returned to traditional values. Under **Ramesses II**, Egypt battled the Hittites in the Levant, reaching a stalemate. Egypt fell into decline, losing control of the Levant and eventually falling to Assyria.

> **QUICK REVIEW**
>
> What were the contributions of the early Middle Eastern civilizations? List several.

INDIA

Meanwhile, early civilizations also developed farther east. The **Indus Valley Civilizations** flourished in the Indian Subcontinent and the Indus and Ganges river basins. The **Harappan** civilization was based in Punjab from around 3000 BCE. The major cities of **Harappa** and **Mohenjo-daro** featured grid systems indicative of detailed urban planning; they may be the earliest planned cities in the world. In addition, Harappan objects found in Mesopotamia reveal trade links between these civilizations.

Later, concurrent with the Roman Empire, the **Gupta Empire** emerged in India. During this period, the Golden Age of India, the region was economically strong. Oceanic trade flourished with China, East Africa, and the Middle East in spices, ivory, silk, cotton, and iron, which was highly profitable as an export.

The Guptas encouraged music, art, architecture, and Sanskrit literature and philosophy. While practitioners of Hinduism, the empire was tolerant of Buddhists and Jains. Organized administration and rule of law made it possible for **Chandragupta II** to govern a large territory throughout the Subcontinent. However, by 550 BCE, invasions from the north by the Huns and internal conflicts within the Subcontinent led to imperial decline.

CHINA

In China, the **Shang dynasty**, the first known dynasty, ruled the **Huang He** or **Yellow River** area around the second millennium BCE and developed the earliest known Chinese writing. Like the early civilizations in the Middle East, the Shang dynasty featured the use of bronze technology, horses, wheeled technology, walled cities, and other developments.

Around 1056 BCE the **Zhou** dynasty emerged and China expanded to the **Chiang Jiang** (Yangtze River) region. Family aristocracies controlled the country in a hierarchy similar to later European feudalism, setting the foundation for hierarchical rule and social stratification.

The concept of the **Mandate of Heaven**, in which the emperor had a divine mandate to rule, emerged. The unstable period toward the end of the Zhou dynasty was known as the **Spring and Autumn Period**; during this time **Confucius** lived (c. 551–479 BCE). His teachings would be the basis for Confucianism, the foundational Chinese philosophy emphasizing harmony and respect for hierarchy.

Following the chaotic **Warring States Period** (c. 475–221 BCE) the short-lived but influential **Qin dynasty** emerged, unifying disparate Chinese civilizations and regions under the first emperor, **Qin Shihuangdi**. This dynasty (221–206 BCE) was characterized by expanded infrastructure, standardization in weights and measures, writing, and currency. The administrative **bureaucracy** established by the emperor was the foundation of Chinese administration until the twentieth century.

> **DID YOU KNOW?**
>
> Shared customs like the use of silkworms, jade, chopsticks, and the practice of Confucianism also indicated early Chinese unity.

Figure 2.2. Great Wall of China

In addition, the emperor constructed the **Great Wall of China**, and his tomb is guarded by the famous **terracotta figurines**. During the Qin dynasty, China expanded as far south as Vietnam.

The **Han dynasty** took over in 206 for the next 300 years (206 BCE–220 CE), retaining Qin administrative organization and adding Confucian ideals of hierarchy and harmony.

THE AMERICAS

Prehistoric peoples migrated to the Americas from Asia during the Paleolithic period, and evidence of their presence dates to at least 13,000 years ago.

From around 1200 BCE, the **Olmec** civilization developed on the Mexican Gulf Coast. Its massive sculptures reflect complex religious and spiritual beliefs. Later civilizations in Mexico included the **Zapotecs**, **Mixtecs**, **Toltecs**, and **Mayas** in the Yucatán peninsula, developing irrigation to expand agriculture.

Meanwhile, in South America, artistic evidence remains of the **Chavin**, **Moche**, and **Nazca** peoples, who preceded the later Inca civilization and empire. The Chavin style influenced later Andean art. The construction of the Nazca lines, enormous sketches engraved in the ground, remains a mystery.

In North America, the ancient mounds in the Mississippi region may be ancient spiritual structures. Precolonial North American peoples are discussed in the US history chapter.

Persia and Greece

The **Persian** emperor **Cyrus** conquered the Babylonians in the sixth century BCE. His son **Darius** extended Persian rule from the Indus Valley to Egypt, and north to Anatolia by about 400 BCE, where the Persians encountered the ancient Greeks. **Greek** (or Hellenic) culture impacted the development of European civilization.

Greece was comprised of city-states like **Athens**, the first known **democracy**, and the military state **Sparta**. Historically these city-states had been rivals; however, they temporarily united against Persia. It was during this period, the **Golden Age** of Greek civilization, that much of the Hellenic art, architecture, and philosophy known today emerged.

QUICK REVIEW

How is Greek philosophy relevant today?

The term *democracy* comes from the Greek word ***demokratia***—"people power." It was participatory rather than representative; officials were chosen by groups rather than elected.

In this period and into the fourth century BCE, the **Parthenon** was built, as were other characteristic examples of ancient Greek sculpture and architecture. **Socrates** began teaching, influencing later philosophers like **Plato** and **Aristotle** who established the basis for modern western philosophical and political thought.

Despite its status as a democracy, Athens was not fully democratic: women did not have a place in politics, and Athenians practiced slavery. Furthermore, those men eligible to participate in political life had to prove that both of their parents were Athenian (the criterion of double descent).

Toward the end of the fifth century BCE, Athens and Sparta were at odds during the **Peloponnesian War** (431–404 BCE), which ultimately crippled the Athenian democracy permanently. Later in the fourth century BCE, Philip II of Macedonia was able to take over most of Greece. His son **Alexander** (later known as Alexander the Great) proceded to conquer Persia, spreading Greek civilization throughout Western and Central Asia.

Rome

Meanwhile, in Italy, the ancient Romans were consolidating their power. The city of **Rome** was founded by the eighth century BCE; it became strong thanks to its importance as a trade route for the Greeks and other Mediterranean peoples. Early Roman culture drew from the **Etruscans**, inhabitants of the Italian peninsula, and the Greeks, from whom it borrowed elements of architecture, art, language, and even religion.

Rome became a republic in 509 BCE and elected lawmakers (senators) to the **Senate**. The Romans developed highly advanced infrastructure and began conquering areas around the Mediterranean, expanding to North Africa.

With conquest of territory and expansion of trade came increased slavery, and working class Romans (**Plebeians**) were displaced; at the same time, the wealthy ruling class (**Patricians**) became more powerful and corrupt. Resulting protest movements led to legislative reform and republican stabilization, strengthening the republic by the first century BCE.

While militarily and economically strong, the republic was increasingly divided between the wealthy ruling class (the **Optimates**) and the discontented working, poor, and military class (the **Populare**). The Senate weakened due to its own corruption, and the leaders **Julius Caesar**, **Pompey**, and **Crassus** took control in a short-lived triumvirate.

Caesar took over and began to transition Rome from a republic to an empire. Caesar was assassinated by a group of senators in 44 BCE; however, in that short time he had been able to consolidate and centralize imperial control. His nephew **Octavian** eventually took control of Rome in 31 BCE. He took the name **Augustus Caesar**, becoming the first Roman emperor.

At this time, Rome reached the height of its power, and the empire enjoyed a period of stability known as the *Pax Romana.* Rome controlled the entire Mediterranean region and lands stretching as far north as Germany and Britain, territory into the Balkans, far into the Middle East, Egypt, North Africa, and Iberia.

Roman Empire

Figure 2.3. Pax Romana

In this time of relative peace and prosperity, Latin literature flourished, as did art, architecture, philosophy, mathematics, science, and international trade throughout Rome and beyond into Asia and Africa. A series of emperors would follow and Rome remained a major world power, but it would never again reach the height of prosperity and stability that it did under Augustus.

It was during the time of Augustus that a Jewish carpenter named Jesus in Palestine began teaching that he was the son of the Jewish God, and that his death would provide salvation for all of humanity. Jesus was eventually crucified; followers of **Jesus Christ**, called Christians, preached his teachings of redemption throughout Rome. Despite the persecution faced by early Christians, **Christianity**'s universal appeal and applicability to people of diverse backgrounds would allow it to spread quickly.

By 300 CE, Rome was in decline. The Christian emperor **Constantine** moved the capital to **Constantinople** and established Christianity as an official religion. The balance of power and stability shifted to the east.

This political shift enabled the western (later, Catholic) church to gain power in Rome. Over time, the Catholic Church would become one of the most powerful political entities in the world; today, there are around one billion Catholics worldwide.

DID YOU KNOW?

These clans and others from Central Asia were able to defeat the Romans in the north and settle in Europe, thanks to their equestrian skills, superior wheels, and iron technology.

The western part of the Roman Empire gradually fell into disarray and succumbed to invading European clans like the **Anglo-Saxons**, the **Franks**, the **Visigoths**, the **Ostrogoths**, and the **Slavs**. The last emperor was killed in Rome in **476 CE**, marking the end of the empire.

Meanwhile the eastern part of the Roman Empire, with its capital at Constantinople, evolved into the **Byzantine Empire**. The Byzantine emperor **Justinian** (527–565 CE) reconquered parts of North Africa, Egypt, and Greece, established rule of law, and reinvigorated trade with China.

He also nurtured Christianity, building the **Hagia Sophia**, the cathedral and center of orthodox Christianity. Over time, a clear schism would emerge between the church in Rome and Christians in Constantinople, creating the Roman Catholic Church and the Greek Orthodox Church.

During the early Middle Ages in Europe and the Byzantine Empire, the roots of another civilization were developing in the Arabian Peninsula. In the seventh century, the Prophet **Muhammad** began teaching **Islam**. Based on the teachings of Judaism and Christianity and following the same god, Islam presented as the final version of these two religions. Like Christianity, it held universal appeal.

SAMPLE QUESTIONS

1) **What is required for a settled community?**

    A.   domesticated animals

    B.   a source of fresh water

    C.   technology

    D.   weapons

    Answer:

    B.   Correct. Fresh water permits a reliable food source, which allows for settlement; people need not travel in search of food.

2) **The earliest known form of alphabetic writing (using characters to create words) is**

    A.   cuneiform, developed by the Egyptians.

    B.   cuneiform, developed by the Sumerians.

    C.   hieroglyphs, developed by the Egyptians.

    D.   hieroglyphs, developed by the Sumerians.

    Answer:

    B.   Correct. The Sumerians developed cuneiform. Hieroglyphs are pictographs.

3) **The Shang and Zhou dynasties are particularly relevant in Chinese history for their contributions in**

    A.   developing Chinese administration.

    B.   centralizing Chinese imperial power as symbolized through the terracotta figurines in the imperial tombs.

    C.   forming a Chinese identity through the development of written language, the Emperor's Mandate of Heaven, and fostering Confucianism.

    D.   ensuring China's safety by building the Great Wall of China.

    Answer:

    C.   Correct. Written Chinese developed under the Shang dynasty, and the Mandate of Heaven emerged under the Zhou dynasty; furthermore, other cultural traditions emerged during these periods.

4)   **The Athenian concept of democracy embraced**

A.   participatory democracy, in which local groups made decisions directly by vote.

B.   an anonymous electoral process similar to that of the United States in which officials were elected.

C.   people of all backgrounds, so that all residents of Athens had a stake in the political process.

D.   an educated electorate in order to ensure the best possible decision-making.

Answer:

A.   Correct. The Athenian notion of *demokratia*, or people power, was participatory rather than representative.

5)   **How did Julius Caesar rise to and retain power?**

A.   He invaded Rome with his armies from Gaul, and used his military resources to control the empire.

B.   He was elected president of the Senate by the people thanks to widespread political support.

C.   He took control of the Senate thanks to his charisma and popularity among the people.

D.   As part of the Triumvirate, he was guaranteed a leadership position.

Answer:

C.   Correct. The Senate's corruption and weakness, and Caesar's popularity with the Populare, enabled him to take and retain control.

FEUDALISM THROUGH THE ERA OF EXPANSION

THE MIDDLE AGES IN EUROPE

The Byzantine Empire remained a strong civilization. Constantinople was a commercial center, strategically located at the Dardanelles, connecting Asian trade routes with Europe. Later, missionaries traveled north to Slavic Russia, spreading Christianity and literacy. Russian Christianity was influenced by Byzantine doctrine, what would become Greek Orthodox Christianity.

Despite the chaos in Western Europe, the church in Rome remained strong, becoming a stabilizing influence. However, differences in doctrine between Rome and Constantinople became too wide to overcome. Beginning in 1054, a series of **schisms** developed between the two. Eventually two entirely separate churches emerged: the **Roman Catholic Church** and the **Greek Orthodox Church**.

In Europe, the early Middle Ages (or *Dark Ages*) from the fall of Rome to about the tenth century, were a chaotic and unsafe time. What protection and stability existed were represented and maintained by the Catholic Church and the feudal system.

Society and economics were characterized by decentralized, local governance, or **feudalism**, a hierarchy where land and protection were offered in exchange for loyalty. Feudalism was the dominant social, economic, and political hierarchy of the European Middle Ages.

In exchange for protection, **vassals** would pledge **fealty**, or **pay homage** to **lords**. Lords were landowners who rewarded their vassals' loyalty with land, or **fiefs**, and protection. Economic and social organization revolved around **manors**, self-sustaining areas possessed by lords but worked by peasants. The peasants were **serfs**. Tied to the land, they worked for the lord in exchange for protection; however they were not obligated to fight. Usually they were also granted some land for their own use. While not true slaves, their lives were effectively controlled by the lord.

Warriors who fought for lords, called **knights**, were rewarded with land and could become lords in their own right. Lords themselves were vassals of other lords; that hierarchy extended upward to kings or the Catholic Church. The Catholic Church itself was a major landowner and political power. In a Europe not yet dominated by sovereign states, the **Pope** was not only a religious leader, but also a military and political one.

Small kingdoms were scattered throughout Europe, and stable trade was difficult to maintain. One exception to the chaos was the Scandinavian **Viking** civilization. From the end of the eighth century until around 1100, the Vikings expanded from Scandinavia thanks to their seafaring skills and technology. The Vikings traded with the Byzantine Empire and European powers. They traveled to and raided parts of Britain, Ireland, France, and Russia.

> **DID YOU KNOW?**
>
> There were limits on sovereign power. In 1215, English barons forced King John to sign the Magna Carta, which protected their property and rights and is the basis of Britain's current parliamentary system.

Meanwhile, by the eighth century the North African **Moors**, part of the expanding Islamic civilization, had entered Iberia and were a threat to Christian Europe. **Charles Martel**, leader of the **Franks** in what is today France, defeated the Moors in 732 CE, stopping further Islamic incursion into Europe. Instability followed Charles Martel's death, however, and **Charlemagne**, the son of a court official, eventually took over the Franks.

Charlemagne was able to maintain Frankish unity, extend Frankish control into Central Europe, and protect the **Papal States** in central Italy. Parts of Western and Central Europe became organized under Charlemagne, who was crowned emperor of the Roman Empire by Pope Leo III in 800 CE. While in retrospect this seems long after the end of Rome, at the time many Europeans still perceived themselves as still part of a Roman Empire. Today Charlemagne's rule is referred to as the **Carolingian Empire**.

Charlemagne brought stability to Western and Central Europe during a period when two powerful, non-Christian, organized civilizations—the Vikings in the north and the Islamic powers in the south—threatened what was left of western Christendom, and when insecurity was growing to the east with the decline of the Byzantines and the emergence of the Islamic Umayyad Caliphate in Damascus. His reign strengthened the Roman Catholic Church and enabled a resurgence of Roman and Christian scholarship.

It was also under Charlemagne that the feudal system became truly organized, bringing more stability to Western Europe. In 962 CE, **Otto I** became emperor of the **Holy Roman Empire** in Central Europe, a confederation of small states which remained an important European power until its dissolution in 1806.

In 1066, **William the Conqueror** left Normandy in northwest France. The **Normans** established feudalism, Christianity, and economic organization in England. Intermarriage and conquest resulted in English control of parts of France, too. Conflict between Britain and France would continue for several centuries, while rulers in Scandinavia and Northwest Europe consolidated power.

The Islamic World and China

Meanwhile, in the wake of the decline of the Byzantine Empire, **Arab-Islamic empires**, characterized by brisk commerce, advancements in technology and learning, and urban development, arose in the Middle East.

Before the rise of Islam in the seventh century, the Arabian Peninsula was located at the intersection of the Byzantine Empire, and the **Sasanians** (Persians), who practiced **Zoroastrianism**. Both of these empires sought to control trade with Central and eastern Asia along the Silk Road as well as with Christian Axum (Ethiopia).

In Arabia itself, Judaism, Christianity, and animist religions were practiced by the Arab majority. The Prophet **Muhammad** was born in Mecca around 570; he began receiving messages from God (Allah), writing them as the **Qur'an**, the Islamic holy book. He preached the religion of **Islam** around 613 as the last, most correct version of the monotheistic religions. Driven from **Mecca** to Medina in 622, Muhammad and his followers recaptured the city and other major Arabian towns by the time of his death, establishing Islam and Arab rule in the region.

Islam appealed to many in the disorganized region. The religion's demands (the **Five Pillars of Islam**) asked followers to declare faith in one god (Allah), pray five times daily, donate 10 percent of their earnings to the community, make a pilgrimage at least once in their lifetimes to Mecca, and fast during the holy month of Ramadan. Anyone could easily convert to the religion, and it brought stability and social organization to a chaotic region and time.

DID YOU KNOW?

A caliph was considered both a political and a religious leader.

After Muhammad's death in **632 CE**, his followers went on to conquer land north into the weakening Byzantine Empire. The Muslim Arabs led incursions into Syria, the Levant, and Mesopotamia, taking over these territories. Thanks to military, bureaucratic, and organizational skill as well as their ability to win over dissatisfied minorities, the Arabs eventually isolated the Byzantines to parts of Anatolia and Constantinople and crushed the Persian Sasanians.

DID YOU KNOW?

Ali's followers called themselves the *party of Ali* or, in Arabic, the *shiat Ali*, which is the origin of the word *Shia* or *Shi'ite* Muslims.

However, disagreements over leadership led to conflict among Muslims and the Sunni-Shi'a Schism. The **Shi'ites**, who centered in Mesopotamia, believed that Muhammad's cousin Ali was the rightful heir to the early Islamic empire. The followers of the Meccan elites became known as **Sunnis**, "orthodox" Muslims with a focus on community rather than genealogy. Over the centuries, other differences would develop.

The **Umayyad Caliphate** (empire), based in Damascus, was named for the leading Meccan tribe that had supported Muhammad from the beginning. By 750, the Arabs would control land from North Africa to the Indus River Valley and Spain (al-Andalus).

Expansion under the Prophet Muhammad, 612 – 632

Expansion under the Rashidun, 632 – 655

Expansion under the Umayyad Caliphate, 661 – 750

Figure 2.4. Islamic Expansion

Ongoing conflict among Arab elites resulted in the **Abbasid Caliphate** in 750 CE. The Umayyads were overthrown by the Arab-Muslim Abbasid family, which established a new capital in Baghdad. The Abbasids professionalized the military, helping consolidate imperial control and improving tax collection.

The administration and stability provided by the caliphates fostered an Arabic literary culture. Stability permitted open trade routes, economic development, and cultural interaction throughout Asia, the Middle East, North Africa, and parts of Europe.

Thanks to the universality of the Arabic language, scientific and medical texts from varying civilizations—Greek, Persian, Indian—could be translated into Arabic and shared throughout the Islamic world. Arab thinkers studied Greek and Persian astronomy and engaged in further research. Arabs studied mathematics from around the world and developed algebra, enabling engineering, technological, artistic, and architectural achievements.

Around this time, the **Song dynasty (960–1276)** controlled most of China. Under the Song, China experienced tremendous development and economic growth. Characterized by increasing urbanization, the Song featured complex administrative rule, including the difficult competitive written examinations required to obtain prestigious bureaucratic positions in government.

Most traditions recognized as Chinese emerged under the Song, including the consumption of tea and rice and common Chinese architecture. The Song engaged not only in overland trade along the Silk Road, exporting silk, tea, ceramics, jade, and other goods, but also sea trade with Korea, Japan, Southeast Asia, India, Arabia, and even East Africa.

CONFLICT AND CULTURAL EXCHANGE

Cultural exchange was not limited to interactions among Christian Europeans, Egyptians, and Levantine Muslims. International commerce was vigorous along the **Silk Road,** the term for trading routes which stretched from the Arab-controlled Eastern Mediterranean to Song dynasty China, where science and learning also blossomed.

Figure 2.5. The Silk Road

The Silk Road reflected the transnational nature of Central Asia. The nomadic culture of Central Asia lent itself to trade among the major civilizations of China, Persia, the Near East, and Europe. Buddhism and Islam spread into China. Chinese, Islamic, and European art, pottery, and goods were interchanged among the three civilizations—early globalization. The Islamic hajj (the pilgrimage to Mecca) spurred cultural interaction, too.

QUICK REVIEW

How did the Silk Road and Islam *both* contribute to global cultural exchange?

Islam also spread along trans-Saharan trade routes into West Africa and the Sahel. Brisk trade between the gold-rich **Kingdom of Ghana** and Muslim traders based in Morocco brought Islam to the region around the eleventh century. The Islamic **Mali Empire** (1235–1500), based farther south in **Timbuktu**, eventually extended beyond the original Ghanaian boundaries to the West African coast and controlled the valuable gold and salt trades. It became a center of learning and commerce. However, by 1500, the **Songhai Empire** had overcome Mali and dominated the Niger River area.

Figure 2.6. Trans-Saharan Trade Routes

Loss of Byzantine territory to the Islamic empires meant loss of Christian lands in the Levant to Muslims. In 1095, the Byzantine Emperor asked **Pope Urban II** for help to defend Jerusalem and protect Christians there. European Christians were easily inspired to fight in what became known as the **First Crusade**. The pope offered lords and knights the chance to keep lands and bounty they conquered. He also offered Crusaders **indulgences**—forgiveness for sins committed in war and guarantees they would enter heaven.

Meanwhile, towards the end of the tenth century, the Abbasid Caliphate was in decline. The Shi'ite **Fatimids** took control of Syria and Egypt, addressing the Shi'ite claim to the caliphate. Other groups took control of provinces in Mesopotamia, Arabia, Spain, and Central Asia.

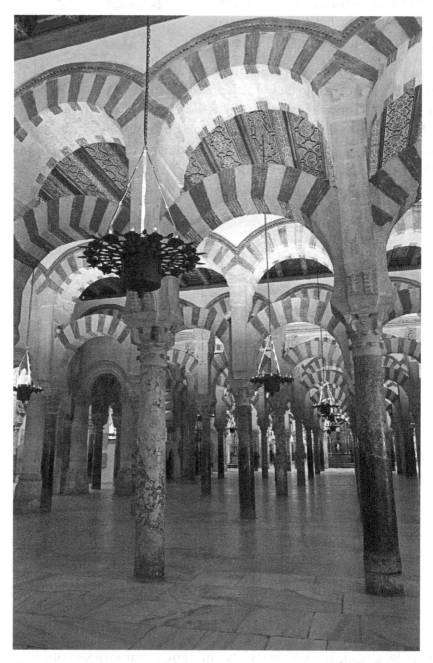

Figure 2.7. Great Mosque Cordoba

Despite conflict in Europe, Christians found they had more in common with each other than with Muslims and united to fight in the Middle East. The decline of the Abbasids had left the Levant vulnerable, and Christian Crusaders established settlements and small kingdoms in Syria and on the eastern Mediterranean coast, conquering major cities and capturing Jerusalem by 1099.

The Crusades continued over several centuries. The Kurdish military leader **Salah al-Din** (Saladin) defeated the Fatimids in Egypt and reconquered Jerusalem in 1187, driving European Christians out for good. Following Salah al-Din's death, the **Mamluks (1250–1517)** controlled Egypt.

> **DID YOU KNOW?**
>
> During the Hundred Years' War, Joan of Arc led the French in the 1429 Battle of Orléans, inspiring French resistance to the English.

While the Crusades never resulted in permanent European control over the Holy Land, they did open up trade routes between Europe and the Middle East, stretching all the way along the Silk Road to China. This increasing interdependence led to the European Renaissance.

Ongoing interactions between Europeans and Muslims exposed Europeans, who could now afford them thanks to international trade, to improved education and goods. However, the **Bubonic (Black) Plague** also spread to Europe as a result of global exchange, killing off a third of its population from 1347–1351. The plague had a worldwide impact: empires fell in its wake.

Back in Europe, conflict reached its height throughout the thirteenth and fourteenth centuries: the **Hundred Years' War** (1337–1453). France was in political chaos, decentralized and at times without a king; suffering the effects of the Black Plague; vulnerable to English attack; and periodically under English rule. While conflict would continue, England lost its last territory in France, Bordeaux, in 1453.

> **DID YOU KNOW?**
>
> Ferdinand and Isabella launched the Inquisition, an extended persecution of Jews and Jewish converts to Christianity who continued to practice Judaism in secret. Muslims were also persecuted and forced to convert to Christianity or be exiled.

In Spain, despite some coexistence between Christians and Muslims under Muslim rule, raids and conflict were ongoing during the lengthy period of the Christian **Reconquista** of Iberia, which did not end until 1492 when Christian powers took Grenada, uniting Spain.

EMPIRES IN TRANSITION

Beyond Egypt and the Levant, the collapse of the Abbasid Caliphate led to instability and decentralization of power in Mesopotamia, Persia, and Central Asia; smaller sultanates (territories ruled by sultans, regional leaders) emerged, and production and economic development declined. **Tang dynasty** China closed its borders and trade on the Silk Road declined. In the eleventh century, the nomadic Seljuks dominated the region from Central Asia through parts of the Levant. However, the Seljuks lacked effective administration or central authority.

Islam remained a unifying force throughout the region, and political instability and decentralization paradoxically allowed local culture to develop, particularly Persian art and literature. Furthermore, Islam was able to thrive during this period: local religious leaders (*ulama*) had taken up community leadership positions, and Islam became a guiding force in law, justice, and social organization. Yet political decentralization ultimately left the region vulnerable to the Mongol invasions of the twelfth and thirteenth centuries.

> **DID YOU KNOW?**
>
> During this period, Persian-influenced Sufi (mystical) Islam and poetry developed; Shi'ite theology and jurisprudence also developed as part of a strengthening independent Shi'ite identity.

In the Near East, the **Mongol invasions** destroyed agriculture, city life and planning, economic patterns and trade routes, and social stability. After some time, new patterns of trade emerged, new cities rose to prominence, and stability allowed prosperity, but the Mongol invasions dealt a blow to confidence in Islam.

Likewise, in China, the Mongols destroyed local infrastructure, including the foundation of Chinese society and administration—the civil service examinations. However, in order to govern the vast territory effectively, the Mongols in China took a different approach. Genghis Khan's grandson **Kublai Khan** conquered China and founded the Mongol **Yuan dynasty** in 1271, maintaining administrative infrastructure and education in the Confucian tradition.

Mongol attempts at imperial expansion in China into Japan and Southeast Asia, coupled with threats from the Black Plague, financial problems, and flooding, led to the decline of the Yuan dynasty and the rise of the Han Chinese **Ming dynasty** in 1368. The Ming reasserted Han Chinese control and continued traditional methods of administration; however the construction of the **Forbidden City**, the home of the Emperor in Beijing, helped consolidate imperial rule. The Ming also encouraged international trade.

Mongol decline was not only isolated to China; in Russia, **Ivan the Great** brought Moscow from Mongol to Slavic Russian control. In the late fifteenth century, Ivan had consolidated Russian power over neighboring Slavic regions. A century later, **Ivan the Terrible** set out to expand Russia further. Named the first **tsar**, or emperor, Ivan reformed government, recognized orthodox Christianity, and reorganized the military. However, overextension of resources and his oppressive entourage, the *oprichnina*, depopulated the state and gave him the reputation as a despotic ruler.

Farther south in Central Asia, the Mongol descendants, **Babur** found the **Mughal Empire** of India. Despite his Mongol roots, Babur identified as Turkic due to his tribal origins, and enjoyed support from the powerful Ottoman Empire in Turkey. In 1525, Babur set out for India. By 1529, he had secured land from Kandahar in the west to Bengal in the east; his grandson, **Akbar**, would consolidate the empire, which at the time consisted of small kingdoms. The Mughals would rule India until the eighteenth century and nominally control parts of the country until British takeover in the nineteenth century.

During Mughal rule in India, the Ming dynasty fell in China and the Qing took over. In 1644, the Ming fell to a peasant revolt; the **Manchu**, a non-Han group from the north, took the opportunity to seize Beijing and take the country. Despite their status as non–Han Chinese, the Manchu were accepted; thus began the **Qing dynasty**, under which China would become the dominant power in East Asia and a successful multiethnic state. They would also be China's last imperial rulers, losing power in 1911.

> **DID YOU KNOW?**
>
> The Mughal emperor Shah Jahan built the Taj Mahal in 1631.

Meanwhile, in Persia, the **Safavids** emerged in 1501. A major rival of the Ottoman Empire, the Safavids were a stabilizing force in Asia. Following Sufism, the Safavids supported art, literature, architecture, and other learning. Their organized administration brought order and stability to Persia throughout their rule, which lasted until 1736, when the **Qajar dynasty** took over.

Despite the instability inland, Indian Ocean trade routes had continued to function since at least the seventh century. These oceanic routes connected the Horn of Africa, the East African Coast, the Arabian Peninsula, Southern Persia, India, Southeast Asia, and China. The ocean acted as a unifying force throughout the region, and the **monsoon winds** permitted Arab, Persian, Indian, and Chinese merchants to travel to East Africa in search of goods such as ivory and gold—and slaves.

Figure 2.8. Indian Ocean Slave Trade

Despite the civilizational achievements of the Islamic empires, Tang and later Ming dynasty China, and the Central Asian and Indian empires that would emerge from the Mongols, the **East African slave trade** remained vigorous until the nineteenth century. Arabs, Asians, and other Africans kidnapped African people and sent them to lives of slavery throughout the Arab world and South Asia. Later, Europeans would take part in the trade, forcing Africans into slavery in colonies throughout South and Southeast Asia, and on plantations in Indian Ocean islands such as Madagascar.

Further north, the Ottoman Turks represented a threat to Central Europe. Controlling most of Anatolia from the late thirteenth century, the Ottomans spread west into the Balkans, consolidating their rule in 1389 at the **Battle of Kosovo**. In 1453 they captured Istanbul, from which the **Ottoman Empire** would come to rule much of the Mediterranean world.

Under the leadership of **Mehmed the Conqueror** in the fifteenth century and his successors, the Ottomans would conquer Pannonia (Hungary), North Africa, the Caucasus, the Levant and Mesopotamian regions, western Arabia, and Egypt. Under **Suleiman the Magnificent** (1520–1566), the **Ottoman Empire** consolidated control over the Balkans, the Middle East, and North Africa and would hold that land until the nineteenth century.

The capture of Istanbul (Constantinople) had represented the true end of the Byzantine Empire; the remaining Christian Byzantines, mainly isolated to coastal Anatolia, Constantinople, and parts of Greece, fled to Italy, bringing Greek, Middle Eastern, and Asian learning with them and enriching the emerging European Renaissance.

The European Renaissance

The **Renaissance**, or *rebirth*, included the revival of ancient Greek and Roman learning, art, and architecture. Not only did the Renaissance inspire new learning and prosperity in Europe, enabling exploration, colonization, profit, and later imperialism, but it also led to scientific and religious questioning and rebellion against the Catholic Church and, later, monarchical governments.

Reinvigoration of classical knowledge was triggered in part by Byzantine refugees from the Ottoman conquest of Constantinople, including scholars who brought Greek and Roman texts to Italy and Western Europe. The fall of Constantinople precipitated the development of **humanism** in Europe, a mode of thought emphasizing human nature, creativity, and an overarching concept of truth in all philosophical systems (the concept of **syncretism**). Emerging in Italy, the seat of the Catholic Church, humanism was supported by some popes, including Leo X. However in the long term it represented a threat to religious, especially Catholic, orthodoxy, however, as it allowed for the questioning of religious teaching. Ultimately humanism would be at the root of the **Reformation** of the sixteenth century.

Art, considered not just a form of expression but also a science in itself, flourished in fifteenth century Italy, particularly in **Florence**. While artists worked throughout Italy and found patrons in the Vatican among other places, the Florentine **Medici family** funded extensive civic projects, construction, décor, and public sculpture throughout Florence, supporting Renaissance art in that city.

Meanwhile, scholars like Galileo, Isaac Newton, and Copernicus made discoveries in what became known as the **Scientific Revolution**, rooted in the scientific knowledge of the Islamic empires, which had been imported through economic and social contact initiated centuries prior in the Crusades. Scientific study and discovery threatened the power of the Church, whose theological teachings were often at odds with scientific findings and logical reasoning.

> **QUICK REVIEW**
>
> The Scientific Revolution changed European thinking. What was the impact of using reason and scientific methodology rather than religion to understand the world?

Also in the mid-fifteenth century, in Northern Europe, **Johann Gutenberg** invented the **printing press**; the first book to be published would be the Bible. With the advent of printing, texts could be more widely and rapidly distributed, and people had more access to information beyond what their leaders told them. Combined with humanism and increased emphasis on secular thought, the power of the Church and of monarchs who ruled by divine right was under threat. Here lay the roots of the **Enlightenment**, the basis for reinvigorated European culture and political thought that would drive its development for the next several centuries—and inspire revolution.

Transnational cultural exchange had also resulted in the transmission of technology to Europe. During the sixteenth century, European seafaring knowledge, navigation, and technology benefitted from Islamic and Asian expertise; European explorers and traders could now venture beyond the Mediterranean. Portuguese and Dutch sailors eventually reached India and China, where they established ties with the Ming Dynasty. Trade was no longer dependent on the Silk Road. Improved technology also empowered Europeans to explore overseas, eventually landing in the Western Hemisphere, heretofore unknown to the peoples of Eurasia and Africa.

MESOAMERICAN AND ANDEAN CIVILIZATIONS

In the Americas, the **Maya**, who preceded the Aztecs in Mesoamerica, came to dominate the Yucatán peninsula around 300. They developed a complex spiritual belief system accompanied by relief art, and built pyramidal temples that still stand today. In addition, they developed a detailed calendar and a written language using pictographs similar to Egyptian hieroglyphs; they studied astronomy and mathematics. Maya political administration was organized under monarchical city-states from around 300 until around 900, when the civilization began to decline.

As smaller Mesoamerican civilizations had weakened and collapsed, the **Aztecs** had come to dominate Mexico and much of Mesoamerica. Their military power and militaristic culture allowed the Aztecs to dominate the region and regional trade. The main city of the Aztec empire, **Tenochtitlan**, was founded in 1325 and, at its height, was a major world city home to several million people.

Aztec civilization was militaristic in nature and divided on a class basis: it included slaves, indentured servants, serfs, an independent priestly class, military, and ruling classes. The Aztecs shared many beliefs with the Mayans; throughout Mesoamerica the same calendar was used. Central in the Aztec religion was worship of the god **Quetzalcoatl**, a feathered snake.

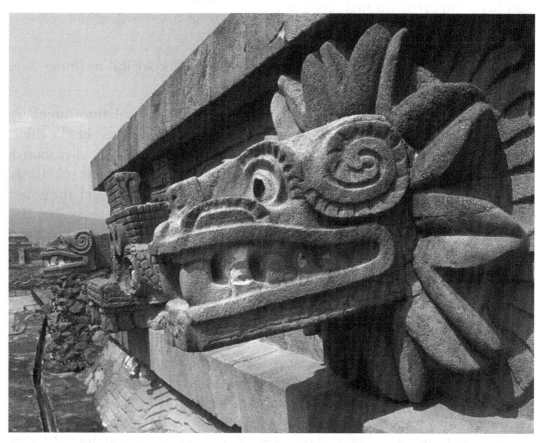

Figure 2.9. Quetzalcoatl

Meanwhile, in the Andes, the **Incas** had emerged. Based in **Cuzco**, the Incas had consolidated their power and strengthened in the area, likely due to a surplus of their staple crop maize, around 1300. They were able to conquer local lords and, later, peoples further south, thanks in part to domesticated llamas and alpacas which allowed the military to transport supplies through the mountains.

Inca engineers built the citadel of **Machu Picchu** and imperial infrastructure, including roads throughout the Andes. Thanks to highly developed mountain agriculture, they were able to grow crops at high altitudes and maintain waystations on the highways stocked with supplies.

COLONIZATION OF THE WESTERN HEMISPHERE

Interest in exploration grew in Europe during the Renaissance period. Technological advancements made complex navigation and long-term sea voyages possible, and economic growth resulting from international trade drove interest in market expansion. Global interdependence got a big push from Spain when King Ferdinand and Queen Isabella agreed to sponsor **Christopher Columbus**'s exploratory voyage in 1492 to find a sea route to Asia, in order to speed up commercial trade there. Instead, he stumbled upon the Western Hemisphere, which was unknown to Europeans, Asians, and Africans to this point.

Columbus landed in the Caribbean; he and later explorers would claim the Caribbean islands and eventually Central and South America for Spain and Portugal. However, those areas were already populated by the major American civilizations. Following bloody conflict with the Aztec and Inca Empires, Spain took over the silver- and gold-rich Mesoamerican and Andean territories, and the Caribbean islands where sugar became an important cash crop.

The economic system that resulted was **mercantilism**, whereby the colonizing or *mother country* took raw materials from the territories for the colonizers' own benefit. Governments amassed wealth through protectionism and increasing exports at the expense of other rising colonial powers. This eventually involved developing goods and then selling them back to those colonized lands at an inflated price.

The *encomienda* system granted European landowners the "right" to hold lands in the Americas and demand labor and tribute from the local inhabitants. Spreading Christianity was another important reason for European expansion. Local civilizations and resources were exploited and destroyed.

QUICK REVIEW

What was destructive about the *encomienda* system?

The **Columbian Exchange** enabled mercantilism to flourish. Conflict and illness brought by the Europeans—especially **smallpox**—decimated the Native Americans, and the Europeans were left without labor to mine the silver and gold or to work the land. **African slavery** was their solution.

Slavery was an ancient institution in many societies worldwide; however, with the Columbian Exchange slavery came to be practiced on a mass scale the likes of which the world had never seen. Throughout Africa and especially on the West African coast, Europeans traded for slaves with some African kingdoms and also raided the land, kidnapping people. European slavers took captured Africans in horrific conditions to the Americas; those who survived were enslaved and forced to work in mining or agriculture for the benefit of expanding European imperial powers.

The Columbian Exchange described the **triangular trade** across the Atlantic: European slavers took kidnapped African people from Africa to the Americas, sold them at auction and exchanged them for sugar and raw materials; these materials were traded in Europe for consumer goods, which were then exchanged in Africa for slaves, and so on.

Enslaved Africans suffered greatly, forced to endure ocean voyages crammed on unsafe, unhygienic ships, sometimes among the dead bodies of other kidnapped people, only to arrive in the Americas to a life of slavery in mines or on plantations. Throughout this period, Africans did resist both on ships and later, in the Americas; **maroon communities** of escaped slaves formed throughout the Western Hemisphere, the **Underground Railroad** in the nineteenth-century United States helped enslaved persons escape the South, and **Toussaint L'Ouverture** led a successful slave rebellion in Haiti, winning independence from the French for that country in 1791.

> **QUICK REVIEW**
>
> Explain the Columbian Exchange.

However, the slave trade continued for centuries. The colonies and later independent countries of the Western Hemisphere continued to practice slavery until the nineteenth century; oppressive legal and social restrictions based on race continue to affect the descendants of slaves to this day throughout the hemisphere.

During the eighteenth century, Spain and Portugal were preeminent powers in global trade thanks to colonization and **imperialism**, the possession and exploitation of land overseas. However, Great Britain became an important presence on the seas; it would later dominate the oceans throughout the nineteenth century.

Though Britain would lose its territories in North America after the American Revolution, it maintained control of the resource-rich West Indies. The kingdom went on to dominate strategic areas in South Africa, New South Wales in Australia, Mauritius in the Indian Ocean, and Madras and Bengal in the Indian Subcontinent, among other places. Later, in the nineteenth century, Britain would expand its empire further. Likewise, France gained territory in North America and in the West Indies; despite losses to Britain in the eighteenth century, that country would also expand its own global empire in the nineteenth century.

SAMPLE QUESTIONS

6) Which of the following explains why the Eastern Roman Empire remained stable and transitioned to the Byzantine Empire while Rome in Western Europe collapsed?

   A. Feudalism contributed to instability in Western Europe, and so that part of the continent disintegrated into a series of small states.

   B. The schism between the Catholic and Greek Orthodox Churches tore the empire apart.

   C. Muslims entered Constantinople and took it from Christian Roman control.

   D. Imprudent alliances in the West led to Roman collapse, while strong leadership and centralization in the East developed a new empire.

Answer:

D.   Correct. Security alliances with Germanic and Gothic tribes left Western Rome vulnerable to their attack; meanwhile in the east, centralized power in Constantinople and strong leadership, particularly under Justinian, led to the rise of the powerful Byzantine Empire.

7) **Following the death of Muhammad, Muslim leadership became so divided that the religious movement eventually split into Sunnis and Shi'ites. This was due to**

    A.   disagreement over succession to his place as leader.

    B.   disagreement about the importance of conquest.

    C.   disagreement over the theological nature of Islam.

    D.   disagreement over whether to accept Christians and Jews as *People of the Book.*

Answer:

A.   Correct. The Meccan elites believed that they should take over leadership of Islam and continue the movement beyond the Arabian Peninsula; however Ali and Fatima, Muhammad's cousin and daughter, believed Ali was Muhammad's rightful successor as his closest living male relative.

8) **Despite the violence of the Crusades, they were also beneficial for Europe in that they**

    A.   resulted in substantial, long-term land gains for European leaders in the Middle East.

    B.   introduced European powers to the concept of nation-states, the dominant form of political organization in the Middle East.

    C.   exposed Europe to Islamic and Asian science, technology, and medicine.

    D.   enhanced tolerance of Islam throughout Europe.

Answer:

C.   Correct. Europeans who traveled to the Levant to fight returned home with beneficial knowledge and technology.

9) **Which of the following was a result of the rise of the Ottoman Turks?**

    A.   Christian Byzantines left Constantinople for Western Europe, bringing classical learning with them.

    B.   The Ottomans were able to conquer the Balkans, the Levant, and eventually North Africa and the Middle East, establishing a large Islamic empire.

    C.   The Ottomans represented an Islamic threat to European Christendom, given their grip on the Balkan Peninsula.

    D.   all of the above

Answer:

D.   Correct. All of the answer choices apply.

10)   **Which of the following best explains the Atlantic Triangular Trade?**

A.   American raw materials were transported to Africa, where they were exchanged for enslaved persons; enslaved persons were taken to the Americas, where they turned raw materials to consumer goods for sale in Europe.

B.   European consumer goods were sold in the Americas at a profit; these goods were also sold in Africa in exchange for raw materials and for enslaved persons, who were taken to the Americas.

C.   European raw materials were sent to the Americas to be transformed into consumer goods by people who had been kidnapped from Africa and enslaved. These consumer goods were then traded in Africa for more slaves.

D.   Enslaved African people were traded in the Americas for raw materials; raw materials harvested by slaves went to Europe where they were utilized and turned to consumer goods; European consumer goods were exchanged in Africa for enslaved people.

Answer:

D.   Correct. American raw materials (like sugar and tobacco) were used in Europe and also turned into consumer goods there. European goods (as well as gold extracted from the Americas) were exchanged in Africa for enslaved persons, who were forced to harvest the raw materials in the Americas.

ARMED CONFLICTS

REFORMATION AND NEW EUROPE

While Spain and Portugal consolidated their hold over territories in the Americas, conflict ensued in Europe. With the cultural changes of the Renaissance, the power of the Catholic Church was threatened; new scientific discoveries and secular Renaissance thought were at odds with many teachings of the Church. The Catholic monk **Martin Luther** wrote a letter of protest to the Pope in 1517 known as the **Ninety-Five Theses**, outlining ways he believed the Church should reform; his ideas gained support, especially among rulers who wanted more power from the Church. Triggering the **Reformation**, or movement for reform of the Church, Luther's ideas led to offshoots of new versions of Christianity in Western Europe, separate from the Orthodox Churches in Russia and Greece. Protestant thinkers like Luther and **John Calvin** addressed particular grievances, condemning the **infallibility** of the Pope (its teaching that the Pope was without fault) and the selling of **indulgences**, or guarantees of entry into heaven.

In Britain, religious and ethnic diversity between Protestant England and Scotland, and Catholic Ireland, made the kingdom unstable. Conflict between Protestants and Catholics was fierce on the Continent as well. The **Thirty Years' War** (1618–1648) began in Central Europe between Protestant nobles in the Holy Roman Empire who disagreed with the strict Catholic **Ferdinand II**, king of Bohemia and eventually archduke of Austria and king of Hungary (what was not under Ottoman domination). Elected Holy Roman Emperor in 1619, Ferdinand II was a leader of the **Counter-Reformation**, attempts at reinforcing Catholic dominance throughout Europe during and after the Reformation in the wake of the Renaissance and related social change. Ferdinand was also closely allied with the Catholic **Hapsburg** Dynasty, which ruled Austria and Spain. Other Protestant-Catholic conflict occurred between Denmark, Sweden, Poland, the Netherlands, and the Papacy.

The tangled alliances between European powers resulted in war between not only France and Spain, but also Sweden and Austria, with the small states of the weakening Holy Roman Empire caught in the middle. The war had been centered on alliances and concerns about the nature of Christianity within different European countries. However, upon signing the 1648 **Treaty of Westphalia**, the European powers agreed to recognize **state sovereignty** and practice **non-interference** in each other's matters—at the expense of family and religious allegiance. 1648 marked a transition into modern international relations when politics and religion would no longer be inexorably intertwined.

The end of the Thirty Years' War represented the end of the notion of the domination of the Catholic Church over Europe and the concept of religious regional dominance, rather than ethnic state divisions. Over the next several centuries, the Church—and religious empires like the Ottomans—would eventually lose control over ethnic groups and their lands, later giving way to smaller **nation-states**.

As state sovereignty became entrenched in European notions of politics, so too did conflict between states. Upon the death of the Hapsburg Holy Roman Emperor **Charles VI** in 1740, the **War of the Austrian Succession** began, a series of Continental wars over who would take over control of the Hapsburg territories. These conflicts would lead to the Seven Years' War.

In 1756 Frederick the Great of Prussia attacked Austria, launching the **Seven Years' War**. In Europe, this war further cemented concepts of state sovereignty and delineated rivalries between European powers engaged in colonial adventure and overseas imperialism—especially Britain and France. It would kick-start British dominance in Asia and also lead to Britain's loss of its North American colonies, nearly bankrupting the Crown.

This time of change in Europe would affect Asia. European concepts of social and political organization became constructed around national sovereignty and nation-states. European economies had become dependent upon colonies and were starting to industrialize, enriching Europe at the expense of its imperial possessions in the Americas, in Africa, and increasingly in Asia.

Industrialization and political organization allowed improved militaries, which put Asian governments at a disadvantage. The major Asian powers—Mughal India, Qing China, the Ottoman Empire, and Safavid (and later, Qajar) Persia—would eventually succumb to European influence or come under direct European control.

THE AGE OF REVOLUTIONS

Monarchies in Europe had been weakened by the conflicts between Catholicism and Protestant faiths; despite European presence and increasing power overseas, as well as its dominance in the Americas, instability made the old order vulnerable. Enlightenment ideals would trigger revolution against **absolute monarchy**. Revolutionary actors drew on the philosophies of enlightenment thinkers like **John Locke**, **Jean-Jacques Rousseau**, and **Montesquieu**, whose beliefs, such as **republicanism**, the **social contract**, the **separation of powers**, and the **rights of man** would drive the Age of Revolutions.

William and Mary defeated James and consolidated Protestant control over England, Scotland, and Ireland under a Protestant constitutional monarchy in the **Glorious Revolution**. The 1689 **English Bill of Rights** established constitutional monarchy, in the spirit of the **Magna Carta**.

The **American Revolution** heavily influenced by Locke, broke out a century later. Please refer to Chapter One, "US History," for details.

The **French Revolution** was the precursor to the end of the feudal order in most of Europe. **King Louis XIV**, the *Sun King* (1643–1715), had consolidated the monarchy in France, taking true political and military power from the nobility. Meanwhile, French Enlightenment thinkers like Jean-Jacques Rousseau, Montesquieu, and **Voltaire** criticized absolute monarchy and the repression of freedom of speech and thought; in 1789, the French Revolution broke out.

The power of the Catholic Church had weakened and the Scientific Revolution and the Enlightenment had fostered social and intellectual change. Colonialism and mercantilism were fueling the growth of an early middle class: people who were not traditionally nobility or landowners under the feudal system were becoming wealthier and more powerful thanks to early capitalism. This class, the **bourgeoisie**, chafed under the rule of the nobility, which had generally inherited land and wealth (while the bourgeoisie earned their wealth in business).

DID YOU KNOW?

Louis XIV built the palace of Versailles to centralize the monarchy—and also to contain and monitor the nobility.

At the same time, panic over dwindling food supplies triggered the **Great Fear** among the enormous population of peasants in July 1789. Suspicion turned to action when the king sent troops to Paris, and on July 14 the people stormed the **Bastille** prison in an event still celebrated in France symbolic of the overthrow of tyranny. Following a period of violence, the monarchy was overthrown.

The French Revolution inspired revolutionary movements throughout Europe and beyond; indeed, the revolutionary principle of self-determination drove revolutionary France to support its ideals abroad.

Ongoing war in Europe and instability in France between republicans and royalists continued to weaken the revolution, but France had military successes in Europe. France had continued its effort to spread the revolution throughout the continent, led by **Napoleon Bonaparte**.

In 1804 Napoleon emerged as emperor of France and proceeded to conquer much of Europe throughout the **Napoleonic Wars**, changing the face of Europe.

By 1815, other European powers had managed to halt France's expansion; at the **Congress of Vienna** in 1815, European powers including Prussia, the Austro-Hungarian Empire, Russia, and Britain agreed on a **balance of power** in Europe. The Congress of Vienna was the first real international peace conference and set the precedent for European political organization.

> **DID YOU KNOW?**
>
> An important tenet of the revolutionary ethos in France was the concept of self-determination, or the right of a people to rule themselves, which threatened rulers fearing revolution in their own countries.

Latin American countries joined Haiti and the United States in revolution against colonial European powers. Inspired by the American and French Revolutions, **Simón Bolivar** led or influenced independence movements in **Venezuela**, **Colombia** (including what is today **Panama**), **Ecuador**, **Peru**, and **Bolivia** in the early part of the nineteenth century.

Figure 2.10. Gran Colombia

EUROPEAN DIVISION

The nineteenth century was a period of change and conflict, and the roots of the major twentieth century conflicts—world war and decolonization—are found in it. Modern European social and political structures and norms, including **nationalism** and the **nation-state**, would begin to emerge. Economic theories based in the Industrial Revolution like **socialism** and eventually **communism** gained traction with the stark class divisions brought on by **urbanization** and industry.

Following the Napoleonic Wars, **Prussia** had come to dominate the German-speaking states that once comprised the Holy Roman Empire. By the nineteenth century and due in part to emphasis on military prowess, Prussia became an important military power and a key ally in the efforts against Napoleon.

Prussia had a particular rivalry with France, having lost several key territories during the Napoleonic Wars. In 1870, the militarily powerful kingdom went to war against France in the **Franco-Prussian War**, during which Prussia took control of **Alsace-Lorraine**, mineral-rich and later essential for industrial development.

Following the Franco-Prussian War, **Otto von Bismarck** unified those linguistically and culturally German states of Central Europe. Prussian power had been growing, fueled by **nationalism** and the **nation-state**, or the idea that individuals with shared experience (including ethnicity, language, religion, and cultural practices) should be unified under one government. In 1871, the **German Empire** became a united state. Bismarck encouraged economic cooperation, instituted army reforms and, perhaps most importantly, created an image of Prussia as a defender of German culture and nationhood, portraying other European states in opposition to that.

The concept of the nation-state spread throughout Central and Eastern Europe, which at the time was controlled by imperial powers like Austria-Hungary and the Ottoman Empire. Nationalism threatened imperial reach. It also led to **Italian Unification**.

IMPERIALISM

As colonialism in the fifteenth and sixteenth centuries had been driven by mercantilism, conquest, and Christian conversion, so was seventeenth, eighteenth and nineteenth century imperialism driven by capitalism, European competition, and conceptions of racial superiority.

Britain and France, historic rivals on the European continent, were also at odds colonizing North America and in overseas trade. During the **Seven Years' War** (1756–1763), considered by many historians to be the first truly global conflict, these two powers fought in Europe and in overseas colonies and interests in North America and Asia.

The **French and Indian War**, as the Seven Years' War is called in North America, resulted in net gains for Britain, which won French colonies in Canada. However, the financial and military strain suffered by Britain in the Seven Years' War made it particularly vulnerable to later rebellion in the Thirteen Colonies, helping the Americans win the Revolutionary War there.

Britain went to war with France in Asia as well. In India, with the decline of the **Mughal Empire** and the rising power of colonial companies specializing in exporting valuable resources like spices and tea, smaller Indian kingdoms were forming alliances with those increasingly influential corporations. By 1803, British interests effectively took control of the Subcontinent and the Mughals were pushed to the north.

Britain would become the strongest naval power in the world and continue to expand its empire, especially in the search for new markets for its manufactured goods to support its industrial economy. During the reign of **Queen Victoria** (1837–1901) the British Empire would expand in Australia, India, and Africa.

Imperial expansion was driven by demand for raw materials for economic growth. The concept of the *white man's burden*, wherein white Europeans were "obligated" to bring their "superior" culture to other civilizations around the globe, also drove imperialist adventure, popularizing it at home in Britain and elsewhere in Europe. Still, other European powers like France, Germany, and even tiny Belgium controlled substantial colonial territory, exploiting natural resources and oppressing the people. Racism was a driving factor in their colonial expansion, too.

> **DID YOU KNOW?**
>
> Major European companies that dominated colonial trade and controlled territory in Asia included the British East India Company, the French East India Company, and the Dutch East India Company.

The European powers were immersed in what became known as the *Scramble for Africa*; the industrial economies of Europe would profit from the natural resources abundant in that continent, and the white man's burden continued to fuel colonization. At the **1884 Berlin Conference**, control over Africa was divided among European powers. Africans were not consulted in this process.

To gain access to closed **Chinese** markets, Britain forced China to buy Indian opium; the **Opium Wars** ended with the **Treaty of Nanking (1842)**. As a consequence, China lost power to Britain and later, other European countries, which gained **spheres of influence**, or areas of China they effectively controlled, and **extraterritoriality**, or privileges in which their citizens were not subject to Chinese law.

> **QUICK REVIEW**
>
> List some of the European powers' justifications for imperialism.

Discontent with the Qing dynasty was growing as Chinese people perceived that their country was coming under control of European imperialists. In 1900, the **Boxer Rebellion**, an uprising led by a Chinese society against the Emperor, was only put down with Western help. Meanwhile, living conditions for Chinese people continued to deteriorate.

In Japan, during the **Meiji Restoration** in 1868, the Emperor Meiji promoted modernization of technology, especially the military. Japan proved itself a world power when it defeated Russia in the **Russo-Japanese War** in 1905, and would play a central role in twentieth century conflict.

INDUSTRIAL REVOLUTION

Throughout this entire period, raw goods fueled European economic growth and development, leading to the **Industrial Revolution** in the nineteenth century. This economic revolution began with textile production in Britain, fueled by cotton from its overseas territories in North America, and later India and Egypt. The first factories were in Manchester, where **urbanization** began as poor people from rural areas flocked to cities in search of higher-paying unskilled jobs in factories.

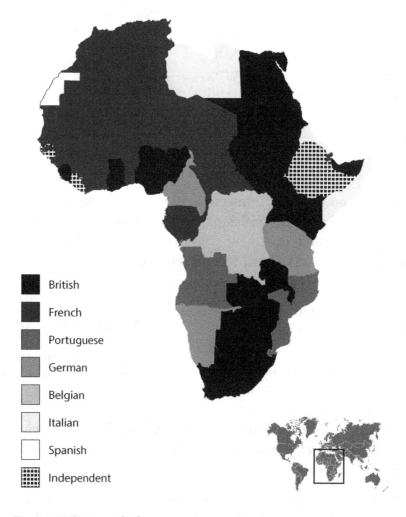

Figure 2.11. Imperial Africa

Early industrial technology sped up the harvesting and transport of crops and their conversion to textiles. This accelerated manufacturing was based on **capitalism**, the *laissez-faire* (or **free market**) theory developed by **Adam Smith**, who believed that an *invisible hand* should guide the marketplace—that government should stay out of the economy regardless of abuses of workers, the environment, or fairness in the marketplace, as the economy would eventually automatically correct for inequalities, price problems, and any other problematic issues.

Technology like the **spinning jenny** and **flying shuttle** exponentially increased the amount of cotton that workers could process into yarn and thread. Iron allowed for stronger machinery and would support the later **Second Industrial Revolution** in the late nineteenth and early twentieth century, which was based on **heavy industry**, railroads, and weapons.

To access the raw materials needed to produce manufactured goods, Britain and other industrializing countries in Western Europe needed resources—hence the drive for imperialism as discussed above. Cotton was harvested in India and Egypt for textile mills, minerals mined in South Africa and the Congo to power metallurgy. Furthermore, as industrialization and urbanization led to the development of early middle classes in Europe and North America, imports of luxury goods like tea, spices, silk, precious metals, and other items from Asia increased to meet consumer demand. Colonial powers also gained by selling manufactured goods back to the colonies from which they had harvested raw materials in the first place, for considerable profit.

Largely unbridled capitalism had led to the conditions of the early Industrial Revolution; workers suffered from abusive treatment, overly long hours, low wages or none at all, and unsafe conditions, including pollution. The German philosophers **Karl Marx** and **Friedrich Engels,** horrified by conditions suffered by industrial workers, developed **socialism**, the philosophy that workers, or the **proletariat,** should own the means of production and reap the profits, rather than the **bourgeoisie**, who had no interest in the rights of the workers at the expense of profit and who did not experience the same conditions.

> **DID YOU KNOW?**
>
> *The Communist Manifesto* contained the famous words *Workers of the world, unite!*

A different version of socialism would later help Russia become a major world power. The Russian intellectuals **Vladimir Lenin** and **Leon Trotsky** would take Marx and Engels's theories further, developing **Marxism-Leninism.** They embraced socialist ideals and believed in revolution; however they felt that **communism** could not be maintained under a democratic governing structure. Lenin supported dictatorship, more precisely the *dictatorship of the proletariat*, paving the way for the political and economic organization of the Soviet Union. The Marxist Social Democrats, made up of the **Bolsheviks**, led by **Lenin**, and the **Mensheviks**, would gain power after the fall of the tsar in the early twentieth century. They would eventually take over the country in 1917.

SAMPLE QUESTIONS

11) **The Treaty of Westphalia**

A.   laid out the final borders of Europe, setting the stage for modern foreign policy.

B.   established the notion of state sovereignty, in which states recognized each other as independent and agreed not to interfere in each other's affairs.

C.   gave the Catholic Church more power in the affairs of Catholic-majority countries.

D.   established the notion of the nation-state, in which culturally and ethnically similar groups would control their own territory as sovereign countries.

Answer:

B.   Correct. The Treaty of Westphalia was based on state sovereignty and non-interference, the core principles of modern international relations.

12) **An important factor leading to the French Revolution was**

A.   the corruption of Louis XIV.

B.   the strong organization of the Estates-General.

C.   support from the United States of America.

D.   the anti-monarchical philosophies of Enlightenment thinkers like Rousseau and Voltaire.

Answer:

D.   Correct. Enlightenment thinking fueled the Age of Revolutions, and revolutionary French thinkers and writers like Rousseau, Voltaire, and others influenced revolutionary French leaders.

13) **Which of the following is NOT a way that the white man's burden influenced imperialism?**

A.   It inspired Europeans to settle overseas in order to improve what they believed to be "backward" places.

B.   Europeans believed in imperialism as in the best interest of native people, who would benefit from adopting European languages and cultural practices.

C.   Europeans believed it burdensome to be forced to tutor non-Europeans in their languages and customs.

D.   Many Europeans supported the construction of schools for colonial subjects and even the development of scholarships for them to study in Europe.

Answer:

C. **Correct.** The idea of the white man's burden was not meant to suggest a literal burden; it was a paternalistic concept of responsibility used to justify imperial dominance.

14) **Marx and Engels believed**

A. that the proletariat must control the means of production to ensure a wageless, classless society to meet the needs of all equitably.

B. in the dictatorship of the proletariat, in which the workers would control the means of production in a non-democratic society.

C. that an organized revolution directed by a small group of leaders was necessary to bring about social change and a socialist society.

D. that the bourgeoisie would willingly give up control of the means of production to the proletariat.

Answer:

A. **Correct.** Marx and Engels believed in abolishing wages and the class structure in exchange for a socialist society where the means of production were commonly held and in which income was equally distributed.

GLOBAL CONFLICTS

WORLD WAR I

Instability in the Balkans and increasing tensions in Europe culminated with the assassination of the Austro-Hungarian Archduke **Franz Ferdinand** by the Serbian nationalist **Gavrilo Princip** in Sarajevo on June 28, 1914. In protest of continuing Austro-Hungarian control over Serbia, Princip's action kicked off the **system of alliances** that had been in place among European powers.

Austria-Hungary declared war on Serbia, and Russia came to Serbia's aid. As an ally of Austria-Hungary, Germany declared war on Russia. Russia's ally France prepared for war; as Germany traversed Belgium to invade France, Belgium pleaded for aid from other European countries and so Britain declared war on Germany.

Germany had been emphasizing military growth since the consolidation and militarization of the empire under Bismarck in the mid-nineteenth century. Now, under **Kaiser Wilhelm II**, who sought expanded territories in Europe and overseas for Germany (including the potential capture of overseas British and French colonies), Germany was a militarized state and an important European power in its own right.

> **DID YOU KNOW?**
>
> The first international war to use industrialized weaponry, WWI was called "the Great War" because battle on such a scale had never before been seen.

In Europe, the 1914 **Battle of the Marne** between Germany and French and British forces defending France resulted in trench warfare that would continue for years, marking the Western Front. At **Gallipoli** in 1915, Australian and New Zealander troops fought the **Ottoman Empire**, allies of Germany, near Istanbul. Later that year, a German submarine, or **U-boat**, sank the *Lusitania*, a passenger ship in the Atlantic, killing many American civilians. In 1916, the **Battle of Verdun**, the longest battle of the war, ended in the failure of the Germans to defeat the French army. In 1916, the British navy pushed back the German navy in the **Battle of Jutland**; despite heavy losses, Britain was able to ensure that German naval power was diminished for the rest of the war. On July 1, 1916, the **Battle of the Somme** became part of an allied effort to repel Germany using artillery to end the stalemate on the Western Front; after four months, however, the front moved only five miles.

Figure 2.12. WWI Alliances

Finally, in 1917, the United States caught the **Zimmerman Telegram**, in which Germany secretly proposed an alliance with Mexico to attack the US. This finally spurred US intervention in the war; despite Russian withdrawal after the Bolshevik Revolution in October 1917, Germany was forced to surrender in the face of invasion by the US-supported allies.

According to the **Schlieffen Plan**, Germany had planned to fight a war on two fronts against both Russia and France. However, Russia's unexpectedly rapid mobilization stretched the German army too thin on the Eastern Front, while it became bogged down in **trench warfare** on the Western Front against the British, French, and later the Americans. Germany lost the war and was punished with the harsh **Treaty of Versailles**, which held it accountable for the entirety of the war. The Treaty brought economic hardship on the country by forcing it to pay **reparations**. Wilhelm was forced to abdicate and never again regained power in Germany. German military failure and consequent economic collapse due to the Treaty of Versailles and later worldwide economic depression set the stage for the rise of fascism and Adolf Hitler.

The Treaty also created the **League of Nations**, an international organization designed to prevent future outbreaks of international war; however, it was largely toothless, especially because the powerful United States did not join.

CHANGE IN THE MIDDLE EAST

The end of WWI also marked the end of the Ottoman Empire, which was officially dissolved in 1923. At the end of the war the Middle East was divided into **mandates**. The borders were decided by the **Sykes-Picot Agreement** between Britain and France, which divided the region into spheres of influence to be controlled by each power, and are essentially those national borders that divide the Middle East today.

In 1917, the secret **Balfour Declaration** promised the Jews an independent state in Palestine, but Western powers did not honor this agreement. In fact it conflicted directly with the Sykes-Picot Agreement, which held that Palestine would be governed internationally. The state of Israel was not established until 1948.

After the First World War, the secular nationalist **Mustafa Ataturk**, one of the Young Turks who pushed a secular, nationalist agenda, kept European powers out of Anatolia and abolished the Caliphate in 1924, establishing modern Turkey.

There was no more Caliph. Refugees and migrants had traveled throughout the Ottoman Empire over the course of the war, suddenly restricted by international borders from their places of origin. People lacked identification papers. Ethnic and religious groups were divided by what would become the borders of the modern Middle East.

The roots of two competing ideologies, **Pan-Arabism** and **Islamism**, developed in this context. According to Pan-Arabism, Arabs and Arabic speakers should be aligned regardless of international borders. Pan-Arabism eventually became an international movement espousing Arab unity in response to European and US influence and presence later in the twentieth century.

Islamism began as a social and political movement. The **Muslim Brotherhood** was established in Egypt in the 1920s, filling social roles that the state had abandoned or could not fill.

DID YOU KNOW?

In 1915, the Ottoman Empire launched a genocide against the Christian Armenian people, part of a campaign to control ethnic groups it believed threatened the Turkish nature of the empire. An estimated 1.5 million Armenians were forcibly removed from their homes and killed. To this day, the Turkish government denies the Armenian Genocide.

Eventually taking a political role, the Muslim Brotherhood's model later inspired groups like Hamas and Hezbollah.

Russian Revolution

By 1917, Russia was suffering from widespread food shortages and economic crisis; morale was low due to conscription and as the military suffered enormous losses and humiliating defeats under the command of Nicholas II. During WWI, this combination of failures at home and on the front only added to widespread dissatisfaction with the rule of the Tsar. The Tsar was forced to abdicate, and a period of violence and instability followed as different factions fought for power.

The communist Bolsheviks, led by Lenin and Trotsky, consolidated their power by nationalizing industry, developing and distributing propaganda portraying themselves as the defenders of Russia against imperialism, and forcefully eliminating dissent. Yet for many, it was more appealing to fight for a new Russia with hope for an improved standard of living than to return to the old times under the Tsar. In the **October Revolution** Lenin, Trotsky, and the Bolsheviks took control of Russia. By 1921, the Bolsheviks were victorious and formed the **Soviet Union** or **Union of Soviet Socialist Republics (USSR)**.

> **DID YOU KNOW?**
>
> In the 1920s, around twenty million Russians were sent to the *gulags*, or prison labor camps, usually in Siberia, thousands of miles from their homes. Millions died.

Following Lenin's death in 1924, the Secretary of the Communist Party, **Josef Stalin**, took power. Under Stalin's totalitarian dictatorship, the USSR became socially and politically repressive; the Communist Party and the military underwent **purges** where any persons who were a potential threat to Stalin's power were imprisoned or executed.

In 1931, Stalin enforced the **collectivization** of land and agriculture in an attempt to consolidate control over the countryside and improve food security. He had the *kulaks*, or landowning peasants, sent to the *gulags*, enabling the government to confiscate their land. By 1939, most farming and land was controlled by the government, and most peasants lived on collective land. However, systemic disorganization in the 1920s and 1930s resulted in famine and food shortages.

Stalin also focused on accelerating industrial development. Targeting heavy industry, these **Five Year Plans** increased production in industrial materials and staples like electricity, petroleum, coal, and iron; they also resulted in the construction of major infrastructure throughout the country from 1929–1938. However, conditions for the workers were dismal. The USSR quickly became an industrial power, but at the expense of millions who lost their lives in purges, forced labor camps, and famine.

CHANGE IN EAST ASIA

Following its victory in the Russo-Japanese War, Japan was recognized as a military power. It joined a world focused on industry and imperialism.

Having already embraced industrialization and modern militarization, Japan turned towards imperialism throughout Asia. In the **First Sino-Japanese War** (1894–1895), Japan gained influence and territory in mainland Asia. This conflict also revealed Chinese military and organizational limitations and showed Japanese military superiority.

Following the First World War, despite having provided assistance to the French and British in Asia, Japan began its own imperialist adventure in East and Southeast Asia not only to gain power and access to raw materials, but also to limit and eventually expel European rule in what Japan considered its *sphere of influence*. In 1931, Japan invaded **Manchuria**, creating the puppet state *Manchukuo*.

Meanwhile, China was undergoing political change. The **Xinhai Revolution** broke out in 1911, resulting in the overthrow of the Qing and the end of dynastic Chinese rule. However, despite Republican recognition by major international powers, the power vacuum left by the end of imperial China allowed the rise of warlords throughout the enormous country, and the government was unable to establish total control.

Figure 2.13. The Long March

The **Kuomintang (KMT)**, or Nationalist Party of the revolutionary government worked to consolidate government power; the KMT leader **Chiang Kai-shek (or Jiang Jieshi)** went on to take control of much of China back from the warlords.

At the same time, communism was emerging in China as a response to western imperialism. Temporarily working together, the KMT and **Chinese Communist Party** CCP were able to bring Chinese territory back under Republican control. However, Chiang turned against the CCP in 1927, driving it south.

The CCP focused its organizing activities in the countryside on the peasants, becoming powerful in southern China. Ongoing KMT attacks forced the CCP to retreat on the **Long March** north. During this time of hardship, **Mao Zedong** emerged as the leader of the movement.

WORLD WAR II

Meanwhile, Germany suffered under the provisions of the Treaty of Versailles. In 1919, a democratic government was established at Weimar—the **Weimar Republic**. Germany was in chaos; the Kaiser had fled and the country was torn apart by war. However, the new government could not bring stability.

Blamed for WWI, Germany owed huge **reparations** according to the treaty to pay for the cost of the war, setting off **hyperinflation** and impoverishing the country and its people. The rise of communists and a workers' party that came to be known as the National Socialist Party, or **Nazi Party**, led to further political instability. Following the crash of the stock market in 1929, German unemployment reached six million; furthermore, the United States had called in its foreign loans. The Nazis, led by **Adolf Hitler**, gained support from business interests, which feared communist power in government.

Hitler maneuvered into the role of chancellor by 1933. His charisma and popular platform—to cancel the Treaty of Versailles—allowed him to rise. Nazi ideals appealed strongly to both industry and the workers in the face of global economic depression. Moreover, the Nazi Minister of Propaganda **Joseph Goebbels** executed an effective propaganda campaign, and would do so throughout Hitler's rule, known as the **Third Reich**.

Taking advantage of a series of crises, Hitler became the undemocratic *Führer*, or *leader*, of Germany, and the Nazis consolidated total control. They also set into motion their agenda of racism and genocide against "non-Aryan" (non-Germanic) or "racially impure" people.

Jewish people were particularly targeted. Germany had a considerable Jewish population; so did the other Central and Eastern European countries that Germany would come to control. Throughout the 1930s, the Nazis passed a series of laws limiting Jewish rights. **Kristallnacht** took place in 1938, an organized series of attacks on Jewish businesses, homes, and places of worship.

In 1939, Jews were forced from their homes into **ghettoes**, isolated and over-crowded urban neighborhoods. Millions of Jewish people were sent to **concentration camps**; the Nazis decided on the **Final Solution** to the "Jewish Question": to murder Jewish people by systematically gassing them at death camps. At least six million European Jews were murdered by the Nazis in the **Holocaust**.

Roma, Slavic people, homosexuals, disabled people, people of color, prisoners of war, communists, and others were also forced into slave labor in concentration camps and murdered there. Later, this concept of torturing and killing people based on their ethnicity in order to exterminate them would become defined as **genocide**.

Hitler was a **fascist**, believing in a mostly free market accompanied by a dictatorial government with a strong military. He sought to restore Germany's power and expand its reach through annexation and conquest. In 1939 Germany invaded **Poland** in what is commonly considered the beginning of the **Second World War**.

> **DID YOU KNOW?**
>
> The Atlantic Charter described values shared by the US and Britain, including restoring self-governance in occupied Europe and liberalizing international trade.

War exploded in Europe in 1939. Hitler gained control of more land than any European power since Napoleon, undefeated until the **Battle of Britain**. Despite staying out of combat, in 1941 the United States provided support and military aid to Britain through the **Lend-Lease Act**.

When Japan joined the **Axis** powers of Germany and Italy, the **Chinese Civil War** between communists and nationalists was interrupted by the Second Sino-Japanese War, when Japan tried to extend its imperial reach deeper into China.

At this time, Chiang was forced to form an alliance with Mao and the two forces worked together against Japan. By the end of the war, the CCP was stronger than ever, with widespread support from many sectors of Chinese society, while the KMT was demoralized and had little popular support.

In December of 1941, Japan, now part of the **Axis** along with Germany and Italy, attacked the United States at Pearl Harbor. Consequently, the US joined the war in Europe and in the Pacific, deploying thousands of troops in both theaters. Meanwhile, Japan continued its imperialist policies throughout Asia, threatening European interests and colonies there.

Back in Europe, having broken a promise to the Soviet Union, Hitler invaded Russia. But in 1942, the USSR defeated Germany at the **Battle of Stalingrad**, a turning point in the war during which the Nazis were forced to turn from the Eastern Front.

In 1944, the Allies invaded France on **D-Day**. While they liberated Paris in August, the costly **Battle of the Bulge** extended into 1945. Despite thousands of American casualties, Hitler's forces were pushed back. In the spring of 1945, when American and Soviet forces entered Germany, the Allies accepted Germany's surrender.

The war in the Pacific would continue, however. An American invasion of Japan would have likely resulted in hundreds of thousands of casualties. To avoid this, 1945, the US bombed the Japanese cities of **Hiroshima** and **Nagasaki** with nuclear weapons in 1945, the only time they have been used in combat. The tremendous civilian casualties did force the Emperor to surrender; at that point, the Second World War came to an end.

Figure 2.14. Japanese Expansion in Asia

That year in China, the Chinese Civil War recommenced; by 1949 the communists had emerged victorious. The KMT withdrew to Taiwan, while Mao and the CCP took over China, which became a communist country.

The extreme horrors of WWII helped develop the concept of **genocide**, or the effort to extinguish an entire group of people because of their ethnicity, and the idea of **human rights**. The **United Nations** was formed, based on the League of Nations, as a body to champion human rights and uphold international security. Its **Security Council** is made up of permanent member states which can intervene militarily in the interests of international stability.

Allied forces took the lead in rebuilding efforts: the US occupied areas in East Asia and Germany, while the Soviet Union remained in Eastern Europe. The Allies had planned to rebuild Europe according to the **Marshall Plan**; however, the USSR occupied eastern European countries, and they came under communist control. The **Cold War** had begun.

THE COLD WAR

At the Yalta Conference in February 1945, Stalin, Churchill, and Roosevelt had agreed upon the division of Germany, the free nature of government in Poland, and free elections in Eastern Europe. However, at the **Potsdam Conference** in July 1945, things had changed. Harry Truman had replaced Franklin D. Roosevelt, who had died in office, and Clement Atlee had replaced Winston Churchill. Stalin felt betrayed by the US use of the atomic bomb; likewise, the US and the British felt that Stalin had violated the agreement at Yalta regarding democracy in Eastern Europe.

Non-communist

Communist

Unaligned

Figure 2.15. Cold War Europe

Stalin ensured that communists came to power in Eastern Europe, setting up satellite states at the Soviet perimeter in violation of the Yalta agreement. The Soviet rationale was to establish a buffer zone following its extraordinarily heavy casualties in WWII—around twenty million. In the words of the British Prime Minister

Winston Churchill, an *iron curtain* had come down across Europe, dividing east from west.

Consequently, western states organized the North Atlantic Treaty Organization or **NATO**, an agreement wherein an attack on one was an attack on all; this treaty provided for **collective security** in the face of the Soviet expansionist threat. The United States adopted a policy of **containment**, the idea that communism should be *contained*, as part of the **Truman Doctrine** of foreign policy.

In response, the Soviet Union created the **Warsaw Pact**, a similar organization consisting of Eastern European communist countries. **Nuclear weapons** raised the stakes of the conflict. The concept of **mutually-assured destruction**, or the understanding that a nuclear strike by one country would result in a response by the other, ultimately destroying the entire world, may have prevented the outbreak of active violence.

Germany itself had been divided into four zones, controlled by Britain, France, the US, and the USSR. Berlin had been divided the same way. Once Britain, France, and the US united their zones into West Germany in 1948 and introduced a new currency, the USSR cut off West Berlin in the **Berlin Blockade**. For nearly a year western powers provided supplies to West Berlin by air in the **Berlin Airlift**. Until 1961, refugees from the Eastern Bloc escaped to West Berlin. Furthermore, West Berlin was a center for Western espionage. In 1961, the USSR, now led by **Nikita Khrushchev**, closed the border and constructed the **Berlin Wall**.

QUICK REVIEW

How did the Cold War erupt between the Allies and the Soviet Union?

Korea had also been divided after the war, controlled by communists north of the **thirty-eighth parallel**. In 1950, the north invaded the south with Russian and Chinese support. According to the Truman Doctrine, communism needed to be contained. Furthermore, according to **domino theory**, if one country became communist, then more would, too, like a row of dominoes falling. Therefore, the United States became involved in the **Korean War** (1950–1953).

UN troops led by the US came to the aid of the South Koreans; China supported the North Koreans. War on the peninsula ended in a stalemate in 1953; tensions continue today.

Later, in **Cuba**, the revolutionary **Fidel Castro** took over in 1959. Allied with the Soviet Union, he allowed missile bases to be constructed in Cuba, which threatened the United States. During the **Cuban Missile Crisis** in 1962, the world came closer than ever to nuclear war when the USSR sent missiles to Cuba. President Kennedy and Premier Khrushchev were able to come to an agreement, and nuclear war was averted.

Despite this success, the United States engaged in a lengthy violent conflict in Southeast Asia. Supporting anti-communist fighters in Vietnam in keeping with containment and domino theory, the United States pursued the **Vietnam War** for almost a decade. The communist **Viet Cong** were waging a guerrilla war against France for independence, and the US became involved in the 1960s when France asked for aid.

Despite being outnumbered, Viet Cong familiarity with the difficult terrain, support from Russia and China, and determination eventually resulted in victory. Bloody guerrilla warfare demoralized the American military, but the 1968 **Tet Offensive** was a turning point. Despite enormous losses, the North Vietnamese won a strategic victory in this coordinated, surprise offensive. Extreme objection to the war within the United States, high casualties, and demoralization eventually resulted in US withdrawal in 1973.

■ Communist countries

Figure 2.16. The Communist World

Toward the end of the 1960s and into the 1970s, the Cold War reached a period of **détente**, or a warming of relations. The US and USSR entered into arms treaties like the **Nuclear Non-Proliferation Treaty** and the **Strategic Arms Limitation Treaty** (**SALT I**). Some cultural exchanges and partnerships in outer space took place.

At the same time, the United States began making diplomatic overtures toward communist China. China and the USSR had difficult relations due to their differing views on the nature of

DID YOU KNOW?

Perhaps the most famous proposal in weapons technology of the Cold War was the Strategic Defense Initiative; popularly known as *Star Wars*, this outer-space based system would have intercepted Soviet intercontinental ballistic missiles.

communism. Following the **Sino-Soviet Split** of the 1960s, China had lost much Soviet support for its modernization programs. Despite advances in agriculture and some industrialization, Mao's programs like the **Great Leap Forward** had harmed the people. In 1972, US President Richard Nixon visited China, establishing relations between the communist government and the United States. Communist China joined the UN.

The climate would change again, however, in the 1970s and 1980s. The US and USSR engaged in proxy wars worldwide. In addition, the **arms race** was underway. President Ronald Reagan focused on weapons development in order to outspend the USSR on military technology.

DECOLONIZATION

Meanwhile, the former colonies of the fallen European colonial powers had won or were in the process of gaining their independence.

In 1949, the Indian leader **Mohandas Gandhi** had led a peaceful independence movement against the British, winning Indian independence. His assassination by Hindu radicals led to conflict between Hindus and Muslims in the **Subcontinent**, resulting in **Partition**, the bloody division of India into Pakistan and eventually Bangladesh.

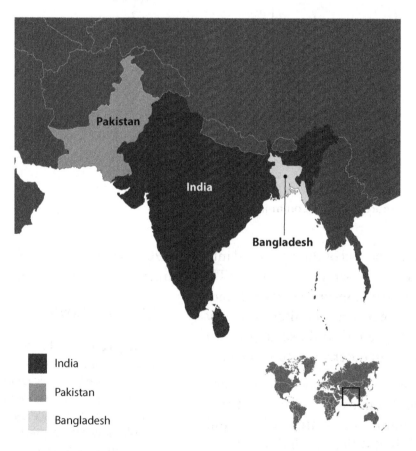

Figure 2.17. Partition

Bloody conflict in Africa like the **Algerian War** against France (1954–1962), the **Mau Mau Rebellion** against the British in Kenya in the 1950s, and violent movements against Belgium in the **Congo** resulted in African independence for many countries in the 1950s, 1960s, and 1970s; likewise, so did strong leadership by African nationalist leaders and thinkers like **Jomo Kenyatta**, **Julius Nyerere**, and **Kwame Nkrumah.** The apartheid regime in South Africa, where segregation between races was legal and people of color lived in oppressive conditions, was not lifted until the 1990s; **Nelson Mandela** led the country in a peaceful transition process.

In the Middle East, the European-controlled protectorates became independent states with arbitrary borders drawn and rulers installed by the Europeans. The creation of the state of **Israel** was especially contentious: in the 1917 **Balfour Declaration**, the British had promised the **Zionist** movement of European Jews a homeland; however, the US assured the Arabs in 1945 that a Jewish state would not be founded there. Israel emerged from confusion, chaos, and tragedy after the Holocaust in Europe, and violence on the ground in Palestine carried out by both Jews and Arabs. The conflict continues in the region today.

DID YOU KNOW?

The revolutionary Iranian government would go on to support Shi'a militants (the *Hezbollah*, or the *Party of God*) in the **Lebanese Civil War** throughout the 1980s; this group is also inspired by Islamism.

In Egypt, **Gamal Abdul Nasser** led the Pan-Arabist movement in the region. Egypt led the unsuccessful **Six Day War** in 1967 against Israel, a major setback for the Arab states. Israel took control of Arab territory. The Arab-Israeli conflict became a Cold War conflict during the 1973 **Yom Kippur War**: the US supported **Israel** and the USSR supported **Syria** and **Egypt**. Conflict continued until 1978, when the American president Jimmy Carter brokered peace between Israel and Egypt (and later, Jordan) in the **Camp David Accords**. By the 1970s, Pan-Arabism was no longer the popular, unifying movement it had once been.

The **Non-Aligned Movement** arose in response to the Cold War. Instead of the bipolar world of the Cold War (one democratic, led by the US, the other communist, led by the USSR), the Non-Aligned Movement sought an alternative: the **Third World**. Non-Aligned or Third World countries wanted to avoid succumbing to the influence of either of the superpowers, and many found a forum in the United Nations in which to strengthen their international profiles.

However, throughout the Cold War, **proxy wars** between the US and the USSR were fought around the world. In the 1980s, the United States began supporting anti-communists in Nicaragua, Afghanistan, Angola, Mozambique, and Ethiopia.

Iran had been under the oppressive regime of the western-supported **Shah Reza Pahlavi** for decades. By the 1970s, the Shah's corrupt, oppressive regime

QUICK REVIEW

Why were proxy wars important in the context of the Cold War?

was extremely unpopular in Iran, but it was propped up by the West. In the 1979 **Iranian Revolution**, diverse forces overthrew the Shah; shortly afterward, Islamist revolutionaries took over the country and established a conservative theocracy led by **Ayatollah Khomeini**.

Following the Iranian Revolution, the Iraqi leader **Saddam Hussein** declared war against Iran. While governed by Sunnis, Iraq was actually a Shi'ite-majority country, and Saddam feared Iran would trigger a similar revolution there. Iraq also sought control over strategic and oil-rich territories. The war raged from 1980–1990.

SAMPLE QUESTIONS

15) **Which of the following was a weakness of the Schlieffen Plan?**

   A.   It overstretched the German army.

   B.   It failed to anticipate a stronger resistance in France.

   C.   It underestimated Russia's ability to mobilize its troops.

   D.   all of the above

   Answer:

   D.   Correct. All of the answer choices are true.

16) **According to the Sykes-Picot Agreement,**

   A.   Israel would become an independent state.

   B.   Husayn ibn Ali would become Caliph.

   C.   Ataturk would lead an independent Turkey.

   D.   Palestine would be under international supervision.

   Answer:

   D.   Correct. Sykes-Picot put Palestine under the supervision of various international powers.

17) **Which of the following led to the rise of the Nazis in early 1930s Germany?**

   A.   the impact of reparations and the support of German industrialists

   B.   the impact of the Great Depression and the support of the workers

   C.   support from the international communist movement and the impact of reparations on the German economy

   D.   support from German industrialists and strong backing from other political factions in the Reichstag

   Answer:

   A.   Correct. The Nazis planned to cease paying reparations, so their nationalist approach appealed to many Germans suffering from the hyperinflation that reparations had triggered. Furthermore, the

Nazis had the support of German industrialists, who feared the rise of communism among the working classes.

18) **The Cold War was rooted in**

   A.   Stalin's unwillingness to cede control of East Berlin to the allies following the fall of the Nazis.

   B.   the erection of the Berlin Wall.

   C.   Stalin's failure to honor the agreement at Yalta, installing communist regimes in Eastern Europe rather than permitting free, democratic elections.

   D.   the Cuban Missile Crisis.

   Answer:

   C.   Correct. The Cold War was rooted in Stalin's creation of communist satellite states in Eastern and Central Europe.

19) **Which of the following precipitated the end of the Cold War?**

   A.   the Iran Hostage Crisis

   B.   the Soviet War in Afghanistan

   C.   the Iran-Iraq War

   D.   the Yom Kippur War

   Answer:

   B.   Correct. The Soviet invasion of Afghanistan and the subsequent ten-year war sapped Soviet financial and military resources—and morale. This draining war, plus the high price of the arms race with the United States, contributed significantly to the fall of the Soviet Union.

POST–COLD WAR WORLD

In 1991, the Soviet Union fell when Soviet Premier **Mikhail Gorbachev**, who had implemented reforms like *glasnost* and *perestroika* (or *openness* and *transparency*), was nearly overthrown in a coup; a movement led by **Boris Yeltsin**, who had been elected president of Russia, stopped the coup. The USSR was dissolved later that year and Yeltsin became president of the Russian Federation. War in Afghanistan and military overspending in an effort to keep up with American military spending had weakened the USSR to the point of collapse, and the Cold War ended.

COLD WAR CONSEQUENCES

In 1990, Saddam Hussein, the leader of Iraq, invaded Kuwait, threatening the global oil supply. In response, the United States and other countries went to war—with a

UN mandate—to regain control of the world's petroleum reserves. The **Gulf War** cemented the US status as the sole superpower.

The changes following the fall of the Iron Curtain led to instability in the Balkans. In 1992, Bosnia declared its independence from the collapsing state of Yugoslavia. Violence broke out, and the **Bosnian War** raged from 1992 to 1995, resulting another European genocide—this time, of Bosnian Muslims.

Also following the Cold War, proxy wars throughout the world and instability in former colonies continued. In 1994, conflict in Central Africa resulted in the **Rwandan Genocide**. In **Zaire**, the country descended into instability following the fall of **Mobutu Sese Seko**, the US-supported dictator, in 1997.

In the 1980s, drought in the Horn of Africa led to widespread famine. The general public became more concerned about providing foreign aid to the suffering. In 1991 **Somalia** was broken up under the control of various warlords and clans; civilians suffered from starvation and violence even after a failed military intervention led by the United States. To this day there is no central government in much of Somalia.

COOPERATION AND CONFLICT

Following the end of the Cold War and post-decolonization, the balance of economic and political power began to change. The **G-20**, the world's twenty most important economic and political powers, includes many former colonies and non-European countries. The **BRICS**—Brazil, Russia, India, China, and South Africa—are recognized as world economic and political leaders.

Steps toward European unification had begun as early as the 1950s; the **European Union**, as it is known today, was formed in 1992. As the former Soviet satellite states moved from communism to more democratic societies and capitalistic economies, more countries partnered with the EU and eventually joined it, with twenty-eight members in 2015 and more in negotiations to join. However, European populism and rejection of globalism is rising: the United Kingdom voted to withdraw from the EU in 2016.

European Union countries remain independent, but they cooperate in international affairs, justice, security and foreign policy, environmental matters, and economic policy. Many also share a common currency, the **euro**.

Continental integration exists beyond Europe. In Africa, the **African Union** is a forum for African countries to organize and align political, military, economic, and other policies. It also organizes peacekeeping missions.

Globalization opened international markets through free-trade agreements like **NAFTA** (the North American Free Trade Agreement) and **Mercosur** (the South American free-trade zone). The **World Trade Organization** oversees international trade. Technological advances like improvements in transportation infrastructure and the **internet** made international communication faster, easier and cheaper.

However, more open borders, reliable international transportation, and faster, easier worldwide communication brought risks, too. The United States was attacked by terrorists on **September 11, 2001**, resulting in thousands of civilian casualties.

Following the attacks on 9/11, the United States attacked Afghanistan as part of the **War on Terror**. Afghanistan's radical Islamist **Taliban** government was providing shelter to the group that took responsibility for the attacks, **al Qaeda**. Led by **Osama bin Laden**, al Qaeda was inspired by Islamism and also by the radical Wahhabism of the Saudis. Bin Laden was killed by the United States in 2011 and control of Afghan security was turned over to the Afghan government in 2014, but the US still maintains a strong military presence in the country.

> **DID YOU KNOW?**
>
> While benefits of international trade include lower prices and more consumer choice, unemployment often increases in more developed countries, and labor and environmental violations are more likely in developing countries.

The Iraq War began in 2003 when the US invaded that country under the faulty premise that Saddam Hussein's regime was involved with al Qaeda and possessed weapons of mass destruction intended for terrorism. The war resulted in thousands of civilian and military casualties, destabilizing the region.

Elsewhere in the Middle East, reform movements began via the 2011 **Arab Spring**. Some dictatorial regimes have been replaced with democratic governments; other countries still experience limited freedoms or even civil unrest. In Syria, unrest erupted into an ongoing civil war. One consequence has been enormous movements of refugees into Europe, a factor in some Europeans' rejection of globalism.

Today, the Islamic State of Iraq and al Sham (**ISIS**) referring to Iraq and Syria (or Islamic State of Iraq and the Levant—ISIL) has arisen. ISIS has established a de facto state in Iraq and Syria with extremist Islamist policies and presents a global terror threat.

SAMPLE QUESTIONS

20) While immediately after the fall of the Soviet Union the US emerged as the sole superpower, in the twenty-first century, which phenomenon has so far characterized global governance?

   A.   international terrorism

   B.   international economic and political organizations

   C.   international conflict

   D.   the European Union

   Answer:

   B.   **Correct.** While the United States remains a leading world power, the emergence of international organizations like the BRICS, the EU, the G-20, and the AU has empowered other countries; furthermore, international trade agreements are helping mold the international balance of power.

21)   **What was one reason for the Bosnian War?**

    A.   attacks by Bosniak Islamic extremists

    B.   the dissolution of Yugoslavia

    C.   the separation of Yugoslavia from the USSR

    D.   attacks by Middle Eastern Islamic extremists

Answer:

    B.   **Correct.** One reason for the Bosnian War was the Yugoslav government's attempt to force the country to stay together; following the end of the Cold War and the collapse of communism, the formerly communist Yugoslavia had started to break up.

22)   **What is one major role that the African Union plays?**

    A.   The AU is a free trade area.

    B.   The AU manages a single currency.

    C.   The AU manages several peacekeeping forces.

    D.   The AU represents individual African countries in international diplomacy.

Answer:

    C.   **Correct.** The AU organizes and manages peacekeeping forces in Africa; it also cooperates with the United Nations in peacekeeping.

23)   **Which of the following is NOT a reason that the Soviet Union collapsed?**

    A.   glasnost

    B.   perestroika

    C.   the war in Afghanistan

    D.   the rise of the Taliban

Answer:

    D.   **Correct.** The Taliban did not emerge in Afghanistan until well after Soviet withdrawal from the country.

24)   **Despite his alliance with the US-supported *mujahideen* in the war in Afghanistan against the Soviets, Osama bin Laden sponsored attacks against the United States because**

    A.   he opposed a US military presence in Saudi Arabia.

    B.   he opposed US support of Israel.

    C.   he wanted to establish a global Islamist regime in accordance with the extremist, unorthodox beliefs rooted in Wahhabism.

    D.   all of the above

Answer:

    D.   **Correct.** Bin Laden cited all of these reasons for his violent acts.

US History

NORTH AMERICA BEFORE EUROPEAN CONTACT

NORTHEASTERN SOCIETIES

Prior to European colonization, diverse Native American societies controlled the continent; they would later come into economic and diplomatic contact, and military conflict, with European colonizers and United States forces and settlers.

Major civilizations that would play an important and ongoing role in North American history included the **Iroquois** and **Algonquin** in the Northeast. Both of those tribes would also be important allies of the English and French, respectively, in future conflicts, in that part of the continent.

The Iroquois actually consisted of five tribes, the **Mohawk**, **Seneca**, **Cayuga**, **Oneida**, and **Onondaga**—which organized into the regionally powerful **Iroquois Confederacy**, bringing stability to the eastern Great Lakes region.

While many Native American, or First Nations, people speak variants of the Algonquin language, the **Algonquin** people themselves have historically been a majority in what is today Quebec and the Great Lakes region. Active in the fur trade, the Algonquin developed important relationships with French colonizers and a rivalry with the Iroquois.

THE MIDWEST

Later, the young United States would come into conflict with the Shawnee, Lenape, Kickapoo, Miami, and other tribes in the Midwestern region of Ohio, Illinois, Indiana, and Michigan in early western expansion. These tribes later formed the **Northwest Confederacy** to fight the United States.

The **Shawnee** were an Algonquin-speaking people based in the Ohio Valley; however their presence extended as far east and south as the present-day Carolinas and Georgia. While socially organized under a matrilineal system, the Shawnee had male kings. Also Algonquin-speaking, the Delaware-based **Lenape** were considered by the Shawnee to be their "grandfathers" and thus accorded respect. Another Algonquin-speaking tribe, the **Kickapoo** were originally from the Great Lakes region but would move throughout present-day Indiana and Wisconsin. The **Miami** moved from Wisconsin to settle and farm in the Ohio Valley. They also took part in the fur trade.

THE SOUTHEAST

In the South, major tribes included the Chickasaw and Choctaw, the descendants of the **Mississippi Mound Builders** or Mississippian cultures, societies that built mounds from around 2,100 to 1,800 years ago as burial tombs or the bases for temples. Both tribes were organized in matrilineal clans, and both spoke Muskogean languages. The **Chickasaw** were based in northern Mississippi and Alabama and western Kentucky and Tennessee; they shared agricultural practices with the Iroquois. The **Choctaw**, whose origins trace to the Deep South and Florida, spoke a similar language to the Chickasaw. These two tribes would later form alliances with the British and French, fighting proxy wars on their behalf.

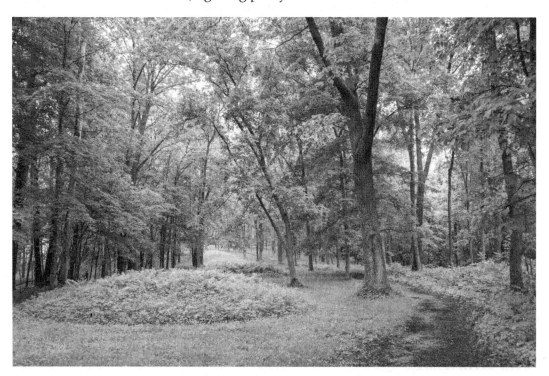

Figure 1.1. Mississippi Mounds

The **Creek**, also descended from the Mississippian peoples, originated in Alabama, Georgia, South Carolina, and Florida. The Muskogean-speaking Creek would later participate in an alliance with the Chickasaw and Choctaw—the Muscogee Confederacy—to engage the United States, which threatened tribal sovereignty.

Unlike the Chickasaw, Choctaw, and Creek, the **Cherokee** spoke (and speak) a language of the Iroquoian family. It is thought that they migrated south to their homeland in present-day Georgia sometime long before European contact, where they remained until they were forcibly removed in 1832. Organized into seven clans, the Cherokee were also hunters and farmers like other tribes in the region, and would later come into contact—and conflict—with European colonizers and the United States of America.

GREAT PLAINS, SOUTHWEST, PACIFIC NORTHWEST

Farther west, tribes of the Great Plains like the **Sioux**, **Cheyenne**, **Apache**, **Comanche**, and **Arapaho** would later come into conflict with American settlers during westward expansion. Traditionally nomadic or semi-nomadic, these tribes depended on the **buffalo** for food and materials; therefore they followed the herds.

In the Southwest, the **Navajo** controlled territory in present-day Arizona, New Mexico, and Utah. The Navajo were descendants of the cliff-dwelling **Ancestral Pueblo** or **Anasazi**, who had settled in the Four Corners area. The Navajo practiced pastoralism and lived in semi-permanent wooden homes called *hogans*. The Navajo had a less hierarchical structure than other Native American societies, and engaged in fewer raids than the Apache to the north.

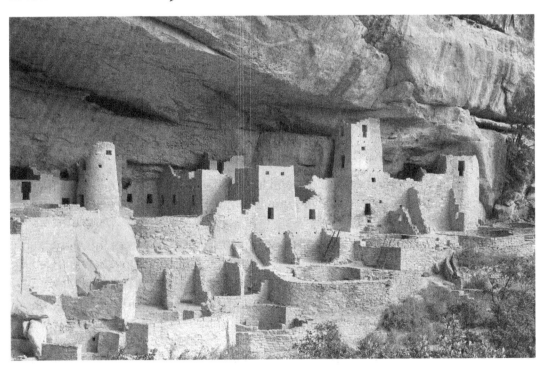

Figure 1.2. Ancestral Pueblo Cliff Palace at Mesa Verde

In the Pacific Northwest, fishing was a major source of sustenance, and Native American peoples created and used canoes to engage in the practice. Totem poles depicted histories. The **Coast Salish**, whose language was widely spoken throughout the region, dominated the Puget Sound and Olympic Peninsula area. Farther south, the **Chinook** controlled the coast at the Columbia River.

Ultimately, through both violent conflict and political means, Native American civilizations lost control of most of their territories and were forced onto reservations by the United States. Negotiations continue today over rights to land and opportunities and reparations for past injustices.

SAMPLE QUESTIONS

1)   **Which of the following best describes the political landscape of the Northeast before European contact?**

A.   Many small, autonomous tribes scattered throughout the region fought over land and resources.

B.   Several organized tribes controlled the region, including a major confederation.

C.   A disorganized political landscape would facilitate European colonial domination.

D.   The land was largely uninhabited, allowing easy exploitation of resources.

Answer:

B.   **Correct.** Powerful tribes controlled trade and territory; among these were the powerful Iroquois Confederacy.

2)   **How do the movements of the tribes of the Northwest (throughout present-day Indiana, Illinois, Ohio, Michigan, and Wisconsin) illustrate tribal interactions before European contact and during colonial times?**

A.   Having been pushed westward by the Iroquois, the Lenape are just one example of forced migration in early North American history.

B.   The migration of the Miami from Ontario to the Ohio Valley illustrates the diffusion of the Algonquin language throughout the continent.

C.   Despite the wide geographic range of the Shawnee, Kickapoo, Miami, and Lenape, all these peoples spoke variants of the Algonquin language; this shows the importance of this language for many Native American tribes whether or not they were Algonquin people.

D.   Ongoing conflict between the Northwest Algonquin Confederacy, based in Ontario and the Upper Midwest, and the Iroquois Confederacy, based in the eastern Great Lakes region and present-day upstate New York, resulted in instability that forced tribes to move throughout the region.

Answer:

C.   **Correct.** While the Algonquin people were primarily located in what is today Quebec and southern Ontario, the Algonquin language was spoken widely throughout North America among both settled and semi-settled non-Algonquin peoples.

3)   **At the time of European contact, the Southeastern United States was mainly populated by**

   A.   the Mississippi Mound Builders.

   B.   settled tribes who spoke Muskogean and Iroquoian languages.

   C.   nomadic tribes who spoke Muskogean and Iroquoian languages.

   D.   the Ancestral Pueblo cliff dwellers.

   Answer:

   B.   Correct. The Choctaw, Creek, Chickasaw, and others were Muskogean-speaking peoples; the Cherokee spoke an Iroquoian language. Both tribes were settled.

4)   **Tribes living in the Great Plains region were dependent on which of the following for survival?**

   A.   buffalo for nutrition and materials for daily necessities

   B.   domesticated horses for hunting and warfare

   C.   access to rivers to engage in the fur trade

   D.   three sisters agriculture

   Answer:

   A.   Correct. The Great Plains tribes depended on buffalo, which were plentiful before European contact and settlement, for food; they also used buffalo parts for clothing and to make necessary items.

5)   **How were the Navajo influenced by the Ancestral Pueblo, or Anasazi?**

   A.   The Navajo continued the practice of pastoralism, herding horses throughout the Southwest.

   B.   The Navajo expanded control over land originally settled by the Ancestral Pueblo.

   C.   The Navajo began building cliff dwellings, improving on the Anasazi practice of living in rounded homes built from wood.

   D.   The Navajo developed a strictly hierarchical society, abandoning the looser organization of the Ancestral Pueblo.

   Answer:

   B.   Correct. The Ancestral Pueblo had settled in what is today the Four Corners region; the Navajo came to control land extending through present-day Arizona, New Mexico, and Utah.

Colonial North America

The Americas were quickly colonized by Europeans after Christopher Columbus first laid claim to them for the Spanish, and the British, French, and Spanish all held territories in North America throughout the sixteenth, seventeenth, eighteenth, and nineteenth centuries.

Spain in the West and Southwest

Spanish *conquistadors* like **Hernando de Soto** and **Francisco Vasquez de Coronado** explored and conquered what is today the southwestern United States. Spanish colonization also meant spreading Christianity, so colonizers established **missions** throughout the region. The Spanish Crown granted *encomiendas*, land grants to individuals to establish settlements, allowing the holder to ranch or mine the land. Colonists demanded tribute and forced labor from local Native peoples, essentially enslaving them, to profit from the land. Spain's holdings ultimately extended through the Southwest, parts of the Rocky Mountains, and California. Spain also controlled the Gulf Coast, including New Orleans and Florida.

Throughout this region, Spanish colonizers encountered resistance from Native Americans. Spain temporarily lost land for two years after the 1680 **Pueblo Revolt**. Sometimes referred to as part of the ongoing **Navajo Wars**, this revolt included several Native American tribes. Spain eventually reconquered the territory, subjugating the peoples living in the region to colonial rule.

The conflict led to friction among Spanish thinkers over the means, and even the notion, of colonization. The priest **Bartolomé de las Casas**, who lived in the Americas, was appalled at the oppression of colonization and argued for the rights and humanity of Native Americans. On the other hand, **Juan de Sepulveda**, who never left Spain, argued that the Native Americans needed the rule and "civilization" brought by Spain, justifying their treatment at the hands of colonizers.

Despite ongoing conflict between Native Americans and Spanish colonizers, there was social mixing among the people. Intermarriage and fraternization resulted in a stratified society based on race in Spanish and Portuguese colonies throughout the Western Hemisphere. According to the *casta* system, race determined an individual's place in the societal hierarchy, with white people most privileged. The term *mestizo* referred to people of mixed white European and Native American, who were more privileged than the Native American peoples.

The Spanish also introduced African people to the Americas. Forced labor and diseases like **smallpox** had decimated Native American populations in Mexico and the Southwest. Consequently, in order to exploit these resource-rich lands, Spanish colonizers took part in the European-driven **trans-Atlantic slave trade**, kidnapping African people or purchasing them on the West African coast, bringing them to the Americas and forcing them into slavery in mines and plantations.

French Hegemony in the Midwest and Northeast

Unlike Spain, which sought not only profit but also to settle the land and convert Native Americans to Christianity, France was mainly focused on trade. **Jacques**

Cartier claimed New France (Quebec) for France in the sixteenth century. French explorers like **Samuel de Champlain** reached land in Vermont, northern New York, and the eastern Great Lakes region, consolidating control of France's North American colonies in 1608.

European demand was high for **fur** and beaver pelts from the Northeast. French colonists were also more likely to establish agreements and intermarry with local Native Americans than other European powers; they did not establish settlements based on forced labor or arrive with families. The term *métis* described mixed-race persons. Eventually France would control the valuable trade routes throughout the Great Lakes and the Mississippi region through Louisiana and New Orleans.

England and the Thirteen Colonies

Unlike the Spanish and French, the English brought their families to North America, with the goal of establishing agricultural settlements. In the sixteenth century, Sir Walter Raleigh established the Roanoke colony in present-day Virginia; while this settlement mysteriously disappeared by 1590, interest in colonization reemerged as **joint-stock companies** sought royal charters to privately develop colonies on the North American Atlantic coast. The first established colony, **Jamestown**, was also located in Virginia, and became so profitable that the Crown took it over in 1624.

Tobacco was the primary cash crop in Virginia. Since tobacco grew on plantations, Virginia required **indentured servants** to farm it. These workers were freed from servitude after a period of work. Some did come from Africa. However in 1660, the **House of Burgesses**, which governed Virginia, declared that all blacks would be lifelong slaves even if they had been indentured servants. The South became increasingly socially stratified, with enslaved persons, indentured servants, landowners, and other classes. The Carolinas and Georgia would also become important sources of tobacco (and rice); South Carolina institutionalized slavery in North America for the next two centuries by adopting the slave codes from Barbados.

While Jamestown and Virginia were populated by diverse groups of settlers, businessmen, indentured servants, and slaves, the demographics were different farther north. In New England, **Separatists**, members of the Church of England who believed it had strayed too far from its theological roots, had come to North America seeking more religious freedom. The first group of Separatists, the Pilgrims, arrived on the *Mayflower* in 1620 and had

> **DID YOU KNOW?**
>
> Slavery was not as widespread in the northern colonies as it was in the South, as the climate in the North did not support plantation agriculture. Demand for slaves was therefore higher in the South, where unskilled labor was needed to harvest tobacco and later, cotton.

drawn up the **Mayflower Compact**, guaranteeing government by the consent of the governed. They were later joined by the **Puritans**, who had been persecuted in England. The colonial Puritan leader **John Winthrop** envisioned the Massachusetts

Bay Colony in the model of the biblical *City upon a Hill*, rooted in unity, peace, and what would be a free, democratic spirit. These philosophies would later inform the American Revolution.

A form of social stratification existed in New England as well: according to Puritan belief, wealth and success showed that one was a member of the **elect**, or privileged by God. Poorer farmers were generally tenant farmers; they did not own land and rarely made a profit.

The concepts of religious tolerance were not isolated to New England. The mid-Atlantic region was well suited for agriculture and trade, with fertile lands and natural harbors. The commercial settlement of New Amsterdam came under English control in 1664 and was renamed New York; in 1682, the Quaker **William Penn** founded the city of Philadelphia. Pennsylvania, New Jersey, and Delaware were founded in the Quaker spirit as part of Penn's **Holy Experiment** to develop settlements based on tolerance.

> DID YOU KNOW?
>
> Quakerism promotes equality, community, non-violence, conflict resolution, and tolerance. These ideas are at the root of the name of Philadelphia, the "City of Brotherly Love."

Earlier in the region, in 1649 the **Maryland Toleration Act** had ensured the political rights of all Christians there, the first law of its kind in the colonies. This was due, in part, to the influence of **Lord Baltimore**, who had been charged by Charles I to found a part of Virginia (to be called Maryland) as a Catholic haven—helping him maintain power in an England divided between Catholics and Protestants.

The North American colonial economy was part of the **Atlantic World**, taking part in the **Triangular Trade** among the Americas, Africa, and Europe, where slaves were exchanged in the Americas for raw materials and goods, raw materials were shipped to Europe to be processed into goods for the benefit of the colonial powers, and these goods were sometimes exchanged for slaves in Africa. In this way, North America was part of the **Columbian Exchange**, the intersection of goods and people throughout the Atlantic World.

Exploitation of colonial resources and the dynamics of the Columbian Exchange supported **mercantilism**, the prevailing economic system: European powers controlled their economies in order to increase global power. Ensuring a beneficial **balance of trade** is essential; the country must export more than it imports. An unlimited supply of desirable goods obtainable at a low cost made this possible, and the colonies offered just that. In this way, European powers would be able to maintain their reserves of gold and silver rather than spending them on imports. Furthermore, those countries that obtained access to more gold and silver—notably, Spain, which gained control of mines in Central America and Mexico—exponentially increased their wealth, dramatically changing the balance of economic power in Europe. Long-term consequences included the decline of feudalism and the rise of capitalism.

Figure 1.3. Triangular Trade

Colonial Conflict

Throughout the chaos in England during the **English Civil War**, policy toward the colonies had been one of **salutary neglect**, allowing them great autonomy. However, stability in England and an emerging culture of independence in the Thirteen Colonies caught the attention of the British Crown. To protect the British mercantilist system, the **Navigation Acts** were enacted in 1651, forbidding colonial trade with any other countries. **Bacon's Rebellion** against the colonial governor of Virginia in 1676 embodied the growing resentment of landowners, who wanted to profit rather than redirect revenue to Britain. Following the 1688 Glorious Revolution in England, many colonists expected more autonomy; however, new leadership continued to limit self-rule.

American colonists were also increasingly influenced by Enlightenment thought. John Locke's *Second Treatise* was published in 1689; critical of absolute monarchy, it became popular in the colonies. Locke's concepts of government by consent of the governed and the natural rights of persons became the bedrock of the United States government. Locke argued for **republicanism**: that the people must come together to create a government for the protection of themselves and their property, thereby giving up some of their natural rights. However, should the government overstep its bounds, the people have the right to overthrow it and replace it.

In the mid-eighteenth century, a sense of religious fervor called the **Great Awakening** spread throughout the colonies; people became devoted to God beyond the confines of traditional Christianity. Many universities were founded during this time to train ministers; the Great Awakening helped develop a more singularly North American religious culture.

Meanwhile, North America served also as a battleground for France and England, already in conflict in Europe and elsewhere. In the mid-seventeenth century, the Algonquin and Iroquois, allied with the French and English, respectively, fought the **Beaver Wars** for control over the fur trade in the northeastern part of the continent. The Iroquois would ultimately push the Shawnee and other tribes associated with the Algonquin from the Northeast and Great Lakes area farther west to present-day Wisconsin.

France had come to control the vast **Louisiana Territory**, from the Ohio Valley area through the Mississippi Valley, the area down the Mississippi River to its capital of New Orleans, and as far as the reaches of the Missouri River and the Arkansas/ Red River stretching west. Not only did France clash with Britain in the northern part of the continent, but the two colonial powers came into conflict in the South as well. In 1736, French forces, allied with the Choctaw, attacked the English-allied Chickasaw as part of France's attempts to strengthen its hold on the southeastern part of North America in the **Chickasaw Wars**.

Figure 1.4. *Join, or Die.*

Following another period of salutary neglect in the colonies, in 1754, French and English conflict exploded once again in North America as fighting broke out in the Ohio Valley. The British government organized with North American colonial leaders to meet at Albany; **Benjamin Franklin** helped organize the defensive Albany Plan of Union and argued for this plan in his newspaper, the *Pennsylvania Gazette*, using the famous illustration *Join, or Die*. However, the Crown worried that this plan allowed for too much colonial independence, adding to tensions between the Thirteen Colonies and England.

The Seven Years' War broke out in Europe in 1756; this conflict between the British and French in North America was known as the **French and Indian War**. War efforts in North America accelerated; ultimately, Britain emerged as the dominant power on the continent. France had allied with the Algonquin, traditional rivals of the British-allied Iroquois. However, following defeats by strong colonial military leaders like **George Washington** and despite its strong alliances and long-term presence on the continent, France eventually surrendered. Britain gained control of French territories in North America—as well as Spanish Florida—in the 1763 **Treaty of Paris** which ended the Seven Years' War.

SAMPLE QUESTIONS

6) **How did Spanish and French colonization in North America differ?**

    A.   Both intermarried with Native Americans; however the Spanish took a more aggressive approach in spreading Christianity.

    B.   Spain sought accord and agreement with Native Americans, while France forced marriages as part of settling the land.

    C.   France colonized the Southwest; Spain colonized the Northeast and Midwest.

    D.   France imported enslaved Africans as part of the Triangular Trade in order to support New France, while Spain mainly exploited the labor of local Native American tribes.

Answer:

    A.   **Correct.** Spain established missions to spread Christianity, in addition to settling and exploiting the land; France worked to establish networks of trade and did not concentrate on religious conversion (although the Church was present and at work in its colonies). Both intermarried locally.

7) **On the Atlantic coast of North America, which of the following contributed to demographic differences between North and South?**

    A.   a climate that supported plantation agriculture in the southern colonies, which resulted in high demand for African slaves

    B.   geography favorable to ports in the Northeast, resulting in diverse and tolerant centers of commerce and trade in Boston, New York, and Philadelphia

    C.   a climate that supported small-scale agriculture and family farms in the northern colonies, which resulted in a very low demand for African slaves

    D.   all of the above

Answer:

D.   Correct. All of the above answer choices are true.

8)   **The mid-Atlantic colonies of Pennsylvania, Delaware, and New Jersey were founded on what premise?**

A.   to be a beacon of unity and humanity, reminiscent of John Winthrop's *City upon a Hill*

B.   to reflect tolerance, as part of William Penn's *Holy Experiment*

C.   to turn a profit, in accordance with their roots in joint-stock companies seeking royal charters

D.   to conquer land and convert Native American tribes to Christianity

Answer:

B.   Correct. William Penn founded these colonies in the spirit of his tolerant Quaker faith.

9)   **How did the British and French rivalry spill over into North America?**

A.   While Britain and France were often on opposite sides in European conflict, they found common ground against Native Americans in North America.

B.   European conflicts between Catholics and Protestants affected Catholic French and Protestant English settlers; related violence from the Hundred Years' War broke out between them as a result.

C.   These European powers engaged in proxy wars, supporting powerful tribes jockeying for control of land in the Great Lakes and southeastern regions of North America.

D.   France and Britain formed an alliance to prevent Spain from moving eastward on the continent.

Answer:

C.   Correct. The Beaver Wars, the Chickasaw Wars, and later the French and Indian War, which was part of the Seven Years' War, are all examples of British-French conflict playing out in North America.

10)   **Which of the following were factors in stirring up colonial discontent?**

A.   Locke's *Second Treatise*

B.   trade restrictions like the Navigation Acts

C.   the Great Awakening

D.   all of the above

Answer:

D.   Correct. All of the above are true.

REVOLUTION AND THE EARLY UNITED STATES

THE AMERICAN REVOLUTION

Despite British victory in the French and Indian War, Britain had gone into debt. Furthermore, there were concerns that the colonies required a stronger military presence following **Pontiac's Rebellion** in 1763. The leader of the **Ottawa** people, Pontiac, led a revolt that extended from the Great Lakes region through the Ohio Valley to Virginia. As this land had been ceded to England from France (lacking any consultation with the native inhabitants) the Ottawa people and other Native Americans resisted further British settlement and fought back against colonial oppression. **King George III** signed the **Proclamation of 1763**, an agreement not to settle land west of the Appalachians, in an effort to make peace; however much settlement continued in practice.

As a result of the war and subsequent unrest, Britain once again discarded its colonial policy of salutary neglect; furthermore, in desperate need of cash, the Crown sought ways to increase its revenue from the colonies.

King George III enforced heavy taxes and restrictive acts in the colonies to generate income for the Crown and punish disobedience. England expanded the **Molasses Act** of 1733, passing the **Sugar Act** in 1764 to raise revenue by taxing sugar and molasses. Sugar was produced in the British West Indies and widely consumed in the Thirteen Colonies. In 1765, Britain enforced the **Quartering Act**, requiring colonists to provide shelter to British troops stationed in the region.

The 1765 **Stamp Act**, the first direct tax on the colonists, triggered more tensions. Any document required a costly stamp, the revenue reverting to the British government. **Patrick Henry** protested the Stamp Act in the Virginia House of Burgesses; the tax was seen as a violation of colonists' rights, given that they did not have direct representation in British Parliament. In Britain, it was argued that the colonists had **virtual representation** and so the Act—and others to follow—were justified.

As a result, colonists began boycotting British goods and engaging in violent protest. **Samuel Adams** led the **Sons and Daughters of Liberty** in violent acts against tax collectors. In response, the Chancellor of the Exchequer Charles Townshend enforced the punitive **Townshend Acts** which imposed more taxes and restrictions on the colonies; customs officers were empowered to search colonists' homes for forbidden goods with **writs of assistance**. **John Dickinson**'s *Letters from a Farmer in Pennsylvania* and Samuel Adams' **Massachusetts Circular Letter** argued for the repeal of the Townshend Acts (which were, indeed, repealed in 1770) and demanded *no taxation without representation*. Samuel Adams continued to stir up rebellion with his **Committees of Correspondence**, which distributed anti-British propaganda.

Protests against the Quartering Act in Boston led to the **Boston Massacre** in 1770, when British troops fired on a crowd of protesters. By 1773, in a climate of continued unrest driven by the Committees of Correspondence, colonists protested the latest taxes on tea levied by the **Tea Act** in the famous **Boston Tea**

Party by dressing as Native Americans and tossing tea off a ship in Boston Harbor. In response, the government passed the **Intolerable Acts**, closing Boston Harbor and bringing Massachusetts back under direct royal control.

In response to the Intolerable Acts, colonial leaders met in Philadelphia at the **First Continental Congress** in 1774 and issued the *Declaration of Rights and Grievances*, presenting colonial concerns to the King, who ignored it. However, violent conflict began in 1775 at **Lexington and Concord**, when American militiamen (**minutemen**) had gathered to resist British efforts to seize weapons and arrest rebels in Concord. On June 17, 1775, the Americans fought the British at the **Battle of Bunker Hill**; despite American losses, the number of casualties the rebels inflicted caused the king to declare that the colonies were in rebellion. Troops were deployed to the colonies; the Siege of Boston began.

> **DID YOU KNOW?**
>
> King George III also hired Hessian mercenaries from Germany to supplement British troops; adding foreign fighters only increased resentment in the colonies and created a stronger sense of independence from Britain.

In May 1775, the **Second Continental Congress** met at Philadelphia to debate the way forward. Debate between the wisdom of continued efforts at compromise and negotiations and declaring independence continued. The king ignored the Congress's *Declaration of the Causes and Necessities of Taking Up Arms*, which asked him to consider again the colonies' objections; he also ignored the **Olive Branch Petition** which sought compromise and an end to hostilities. **Thomas Paine** published his pamphlet *Common Sense*; taking Locke's concepts of natural rights and the obligation of a people to rebel against an oppressive government, it popularized the notion of rebellion against Britain.

By summer of 1776, the Continental Congress agreed on the need to break from Britain; on July 4, 1776, it declared the independence of the United States of America and issued the **Declaration of Independence**, drafted mainly by **Thomas Jefferson** and heavily influenced by Locke.

Americans were still divided over independence; **Patriots** favored independence while those still loyal to Britain were known as **Tories. George Washington** had been appointed head of the Continental Army and led a largely unpaid and unprofessional army; despite early losses, Washington gained ground due to strong leadership, superior knowledge of the land, and support from France (and to a lesser extent, Spain and the Netherlands). The tide turned in 1777 at **Valley Forge**, when Washington and his army lived through the bitterly cold winter and managed to overcome British military forces. The British people did not favor the war and voted the Tories out of Parliament; the incoming Whig party sought to end the war. In the 1783 **Treaty of Paris**, the United States was recognized as a country, agreeing to repay debts to British merchants and provide safety to those British loyalists who wished to remain in North America. The American Revolution would go on to inspire revolution around the world.

Federalists and Democratic-Republicans

Joy in victory was short-lived. Fearful of tyranny, the Second Continental Congress had authorized only a weak central government, adopting the **Articles of Confederation** to organize the Thirteen Colonies—now states—into a loosely united country. A unicameral central government had the power to wage war, negotiate treaties, and borrow money. It could not tax citizens, but it could tax states. It also set parameters for westward expansion and establishing new states: the **Northwest Ordinances** of 1787 forbade slavery north of the Ohio River. Areas with 60,000 people could apply for statehood. However, it soon became clear that the Articles of Confederation were not strong enough to keep the nation united.

The new country was heavily in debt. Currency was weak, taxes were high, and instability loomed. Daniel Shays led **Shays' Rebellion**, a revolt of indebted farmers who sought to prevent courts from seizing property in Massachusetts and to protest debtor's prisons. Furthermore, debt and disorganization made the country appear weak and vulnerable to Great Britain and Spain. If the United States was to remain one country, it needed a stronger federal government.

> **DID YOU KNOW?**
>
> The Northwest Ordinances also effectively nullified King George III's Proclamation of 1763, which promised Native Americans that white settlement would not continue in the Ohio Valley region. The United States did not recognize the Proclamation, and tensions would build.

Alexander Hamilton and **James Madison** called for a **Constitutional Convention** to frame a stronger federal government in a written constitution. Madison and other **Federalists** like **John Adams** believed in **separation of powers**, republicanism, and a strong federal government.

To determine the exact structure of the government, delegates at the convention settled on what became known as the **Great Compromise**, a **bicameral legislature**. Two plans had been presented: the **New Jersey Plan**, which proposed a legislature composed of an equal number of representatives from each state (which would benefit smaller states), and the **Virginia Plan**, which proposed a legislature composed of representatives proportional to the population of each state. States with large populations of enslaved African Americans accounted for those persons with the **Three-Fifths Compromise**, which counted a slave as three-fifths of a person. While represented in a state's population to determine that state's representation in Congress, enslaved persons had no place in the political process. The states adopted both plans, creating the **House of Representatives** and the **Senate**, to represent the large and small states at the federal level.

Despite the separation of powers provided for in the Constitution, **Anti-Federalists** like **Thomas Jefferson** called for even more limitations on the power of the federal government. The first ten amendments to the Constitution, or the **Bill of Rights**, a list of guarantees of American freedoms, was a concession to the

Anti-Federalists, who would later become the **Democratic-Republican Party** (eventually, the Democratic Party).

To convince the states of the benefits of federalism and to ratify the Constitution, Hamilton, Madison, and John Jay wrote the *Federalist Papers*. Likewise, the Bill of Rights helped sway the hesitant. In 1791, the Constitution was ratified. **George Washington** was elected president, with John Adams serving as vice president; Washington appointed Hamilton as Secretary of the Treasury and Jefferson as Secretary of State.

Hamilton prioritized currency stabilization and repayment of debts; he also believed in establishing a national bank—the **Bank of the United States (BUS)**. He also favored tariffs and excise (sales) taxes, which Anti-Federalists—who became known as **Democratic-Republicans**—vehemently opposed. in 1795, rebellion against the excise tax on whiskey broke out; the **Whiskey Rebellion** indicated unrest in the young country and was put down by militia.

President Washington issued the **Neutrality Proclamation** in 1793, keeping the US out of the French Revolution. However, British and French ships accosted American ships in the Atlantic and forced American sailors into naval service (**impressment**). **Jay's Treaty**, an attempt at reinstating neutrality, was unsuccessful and unpopular; it only negotiated the removal of British forts in the western frontier. Furthermore, Spain became concerned about changes in the continental balance of power. President Washington had Thomas Pickney negotiate a new treaty with Spain; giving the US rights on the Mississippi River and in the Port of New Orleans, **Pickney's Treaty** was a diplomatic success and ratified by all thirteen states. The **Northwest Indian Wars** continued in the Ohio region; ultimately the Americans gained territory in Ohio and Indiana following the defeat of allied tribes at the **Battle of Fallen Timbers** in 1794.

DID YOU KNOW?

Federalists were generally from the North and were usually merchants or businessmen; Anti-Federalists were usually from the South or the rural west, and farmed the land.

In President Washington's **Farewell Address**, he recommended the United States adhere to neutrality in international affairs, setting a precedent for early American history. Vice President John Adams, a Federalist, became the second president. France continued to seize American ships, so Adams sent representatives to negotiate; however, in what became known as the **XYZ Affair**, the Americans were asked for bribes in order to even meet with French officials. The insulted Americans began an undeclared conflict in the Caribbean until the **Convention of 1800** negotiated a cessation of hostilities.

During the Adams administration, the Federalists passed the harsh **Alien and Sedition Acts**. The Alien Act allowed the president to deport "enemy aliens"; it also increased the residency requirements for citizenship. The Sedition Act forbade criticism of the president or of Congress. Divisions between the Federalists and the Democratic-Republicans were deeper than ever and the presidential elections of 1800 were tense and controversial. Nevertheless, Thomas Jefferson was elected to the presidency in 1801 in a non-violent transfer of power.

Jefferson repealed the Alien and Sedition Acts and shrank the federal government. Economic policies favored small farmers and landowners, in contrast to Federalist policies, which supported big business and cities. However, Jefferson also oversaw the **Louisiana Purchase**, which nearly doubled the size of the United States. This troubled some Democratic-Republicans, who saw this as federal overreach, but the Louisiana Purchase would be a major step in westward expansion.

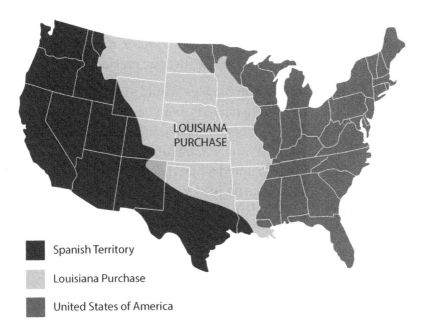

Figure 1.5. Louisiana Purchase

Jefferson was also forced to manage chaotic international affairs. Britain and France, at war in Europe, were attempting to blockade each other's international trade, threatening US ships and commerce. In an attempt to avoid the conflict, Congress passed the **Embargo Act** in 1807, restricting international trade. However this law only damaged the US economy further. At the end of Jefferson's presidency, Congress passed the **Non-Intercourse Act**, which allowed trade with foreign countries besides Britain and France; under President **James Madison**, tensions would remain high.

MONROE DOCTRINE AND MANIFEST DESTINY

British provocation at sea and in the northwest led to the **War of 1812**. Growing nationalism in the United States pressured Madison into pushing for war after the **Battle of Tippecanoe** in Indiana, when **General William Henry Harrison** fought the **Northwest Confederacy**, a group of tribes led by the Shawnee leader **Tecumseh**. The Shawnee, Lenape, Miami, Kickapoo, and others had come together not only out of common interest—to maintain control over their lands—but also because they followed Tecumseh's brother **Tenskwatawa**, who was considered a prophet.

Despite the Confederacy's alliance with Britain, the United States prevailed. Congress declared war with the intent to defend the United States, end commercial disruption and impressment of Americans at sea, and destabilize British Canada. The war resulted in no real gains or losses for either the Americans or the British. Yet at the war's end, the United States had successfully reaffirmed its independence. The Federalists, who had opposed the war, eventually collapsed. Patriotism ran high.

The **Era of Good Feelings** began with the presidency of **James Monroe** as a strong sense of public identity and nationalism pervaded in the country. In a religious revival called the **Second Great Awakening**, people turned from Puritanism to Baptist and Methodist faiths, following revolutionary preachers and movements. In art and culture, romanticism and reform movements elevated the "common man," a trend that would continue into the presidency of Andrew Jackson.

From a financial perspective, the country would again struggle. Disagreement over the **Tariff of 1816** divided industrialists, who believed in nurturing American industry, from Southern landowners, who depended on exporting cotton and tobacco for profit. Later, following the establishment of the **Second Bank of the United States**, the **Panic of 1819** erupted when the government cut credit following overspeculation on western lands; the BUS wanted payment from state banks in hard currency, or **specie**. Western banks foreclosed on western farmers.

With the Louisiana Purchase, the country had almost doubled in size. In the nineteenth century, the idea of **manifest destiny**, or the sense that it was the fate of the United States to expand westward and settle the continent, prevailed. Also in 1819, the United States purchased Florida from Spain in the **Adams-Onis Treaty**. The **Monroe Doctrine**, James Monroe's policy that the Western Hemisphere was "closed" to any further European colonization or exploration, asserted US hegemony in the region.

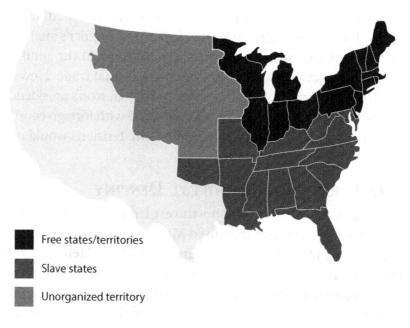

Free states/territories

Slave states

Unorganized territory

Figure 1.6. Missouri Compromise

Westward expansion triggered questions about the expansion of slavery, a divisive issue. Slavery was profitable for the southern states which depended on the plantation economy, but increasingly condemned in the North. Furthermore, the Second Great Awakening had fueled the **abolitionist** movement. In debating the nature of westward expansion, the Kentucky senator **Henry Clay** worked out a compromise. The **Missouri Compromise**, also known as the **Compromise of 1820**, allowed Missouri to join the union as a slave state, but provided that any other states north of the **thirty-sixth parallel (36°30')** would be free. Maine would also join the nation as a free state. However, more tension and compromises over the nature of slavery in the West were to come.

JACKSONIAN DEMOCRACY

Demographics were changing throughout the early nineteenth century. Technological advances had increased cotton yield; therefore, more persons were enslaved than ever before, bringing more urgency to the issue of slavery. In addition, **immigration** from Europe to the United States was increasing. Reactionary **nativist** movements like the **Know-Nothing Party** feared the influx of non-Anglo Europeans, particularly Catholics, and discrimination was widespread, especially against the Irish. Other technological advances like the **railroads** and **steamships** were speeding up westward expansion and improving trade throughout the continent; a large-scale **market economy** was emerging. With early industrialization and changing concepts following the Second Great Awakening, women were playing a larger role in society, even though they could not vote.

Most states had extended voting rights to white men who did not own land or substantial property: **universal manhood suffrage**. Elected officials would increasingly come to better reflect the electorate, and the brash war hero Jackson was popular among the "common man."

During the election of 1824, Andrew Jackson ran against **John Quincy Adams**, Henry Clay, and William Crawford, all Republicans (from the Democratic-Republican party); John Quincy Adams won. By 1828, divisions within the party had Jackson and his supporters known as Democrats, in favor of small farmers and inhabitants of rural areas, and states' rights. Clay and his supporters became known as **National Republicans** and, later, **Whigs**, a splinter group of the Democratic-Republicans which supported business and urbanization; they also had federalist leanings. Thus the **two-party system** emerged.

Andrew Jackson's popularity with the "common man," white, male farmers and workers who felt he identified with them, and the fact that owning property was no longer a requirement to vote, gave him the advantage and a two-term presidency. Jackson rewarded his supporters, appointing them to important positions as part of the **spoils system**.

Opposed to the Bank of the United States, he issued the **Specie Circular**, devaluing paper money and instigating the financial **Panic of 1837**. Despite his opposition to such deep federal economic control, Jackson was forced to contend with controversial tariffs. The **Tariff of 1828**, or **Tariff of Abominations**, benefitted northern industry, but heavily affected southern exports. Senator **John C. Calhoun** of South Carolina argued for **nullification**, the right of a state to declare a law null and void if it was harmful.

Tensions increased with the **Tariff of 1832**; Calhoun and South Carolina threatened to secede if their economic interests were not protected. Jackson managed the **Nullification Crisis** without resorting to violence, working out a compromise in 1833 that was more favorable to the South.

Socially and politically, white men of varying levels of economic success and education had stronger political voices and more opportunities in civil society. However, women, African Americans, and Native Americans did not. With continental expansion came conflict with Native Americans. Despite efforts by the Cherokee, who unsuccessfully argued for the right to their land in the Supreme Court case *Cherokee Nation v. Georgia* (1831), President Jackson enforced the 1830 **Indian Removal Act**, forcing tribes from their lands in the Southeast. Thousands of people were forced to travel mainly on foot, with all of their belongings, to Indian Territory (today, Oklahoma) on the infamous **Trail of Tears**, to make way for white settlers. Violent conflicts would continue on the Frontier farther west between the US and the Apache, Comanche, Sioux, Arapaho, Cheyenne, and other tribes throughout the nineteenth century.

SAMPLE QUESTIONS

11) **How did the Quartering Act impact the colonists?**

    A. Colonists were forced to take British soldiers into their homes; protests against the Act led to the Boston Tea Party.

    B. Colonists were forced to build quarters for British soldiers who were stationed locally.

    C. Colonists had to provide one-quarter of their earnings to support British soldiers stationed locally.

    D. Colonists were forced to take British soldiers into their homes; protests against the Act led to the Boston Massacre.

Answer:

   D.   Correct. Anger at being forced to provide shelter for British soldiers led to protests; in 1770, British soldiers fired on protests against the Quartering Act in what came to be called the Boston Massacre.

12) **What was the impact of Shays' Rebellion?**

A. It showed resistance to imposing excise taxes on whiskey and other consumer goods.

B. It illustrated the need for a stronger federal government in the young United States.

C. Taxes engineered by Hamilton during the Washington administration were cut.

D. The radical Democratic-Republicans emerged to protest the Bank of the United States.

Answer:

B. Correct. Shays' Rebellion, in which Daniel Shays led a rebellion of indebted farmers shortly after the end of the Revolution, showed the need for a stronger federal government to ensure national stability and was a major factor in planning the Constitutional Convention.

13) **What was the impact of United States' rejection of the Proclamation of 1763?**

A. A series of conflicts between the Americans and the Northwest tribes (later, the Northwest Confederacy) culminated in the War of 1812. Ultimately, the US would control the land.

B. The French and British formed the Northwest Confederacy, allying against the United States to control more land in North America.

C. A series of conflicts between the Americans and the Northwest tribes culminated in the War of 1812. Ultimately, the Northwest Confederacy would control the land for another century before ceding it to Canada.

D. The Northwest Confederacy of British and American soldiers united to drive Native American tribes from what is today the Midwest region of the United States, allowing whites to establish settlements there.

Answer:

A. Correct. Despite efforts by the tribes to retain control over their land, they would eventually lose a series of conflicts and the United States would establish states in the Midwest and Ohio Valley region.

14) **How did the Missouri Compromise reflect divisions over slavery?**

A. It showed disagreement over the nature of westward expansion.

B. It showed the impact of the abolitionist movement on politics.

C. It showed how the Second Great Awakening had influenced society.

D. all of the above

Answer:

D. Correct. All of the answer choices are true.

15) **How did demographics play a part in democratic change during the early and mid-nineteenth century, particularly in the context of Jacksonian Democracy?**

A.   The rising strength of industry in the Northeast, coupled with the beginnings of railroads, strengthened support for pro-business politicians and the business class.

B.   Wealthy European immigrants shifted the balance of power away from the "common man" to business owners and the elites, leading to the rise of the powerful Whig party.

C.   Universal manhood suffrage shifted the balance of political power away from the elites; immigration accelerated westward expansion and began to power early industry and urban development.

D.   Jackson's focus on strengthening the federal government dissatisfied the South, leading to the Nullification Crisis.

Answer:

C.   **Correct.** Universal manhood suffrage allowed all white males, whether or not they owned property, to vote; the "common man" had a voice in government, and Jackson enjoyed their support. Likewise, an influx of poor European immigrants changed the country's demographics, providing more workers for early industry, more settlers to populate the west, and a stronger voice in government against the wealthy.

CIVIL WAR, EXPANSION, AND INDUSTRY

THE ROAD TO CONFLICT

The Civil War was rooted in ongoing conflict over slavery, states' rights, and the reach of the federal government. Reform movements of the mid-nineteenth century fueled the abolitionist movement. The Missouri Compromise and the Nullification Crisis foreshadowed worsening division to come.

In 1836, Texas, where there were a great number of white settlers, declared independence from Mexico. In 1845, Texas joined the Union; this event, in addition to US hunger for land, triggered the **Mexican-American War**. As a result of the **Treaty of Guadalupe Hidalgo**, which ended the war following Mexico's surrender, the United States obtained territory in the Southwest and gold-rich California. The population of California would grow rapidly with the **gold rush** as prospectors headed west to try their fortunes. However, Hispanics who had lived in the region under Mexico lost their land and were denied many of the rights that whites enjoyed—even though they had been promised US citizenship and equal rights under the treaty. They also suffered from racial discrimination.

Meanwhile, social change in the Northeast and growing Midwest continued. As the market economy and early industry developed, so did the **middle class**. The role of **women** changed; extra income allowed many to stay at home. The

Cult of Domesticity, a popular cultural movement, encouraged women to become homemakers and focus on domestic skills. However, women were also freed up to engage in social activism. Activists like **Susan B. Anthony** and **Elizabeth Cady Stanton** worked for women's rights, including women's suffrage, culminating in the 1848 **Seneca Falls Convention** led by the **American Woman Suffrage Association**. Women were also active in the temperance movement. Organizations like the Woman's Christian Temperance Union advocated for the prohibition of alcohol, which was finally achieved with the Eighteenth Amendment, although it was later repealed with the Twenty-First.

Reform movements continued to include abolitionism, which ranged from moderate to radical. The American Colonization Society wanted to end slavery and send former slaves to Africa. The activist, writer, and former slave **Frederick Douglass** advocated for **abolition**. Douglass publicized the movement along with the American Anti-Slavery Society and publications like Harriet Beecher Stowe's *Uncle Tom's Cabin*. The radical abolitionist **John Brown** led violent protests against slavery. Abolitionism became a key social and political issue.

The industrial change in the North did not extend to the South, which continued to rely on plantations and cotton exports. Nor were the majority of demographic changes occurring in the South. Differences among the regions grew, and disputes over extending slavery into new southwestern territories obtained from Mexico continued. Another compromise was needed.

Anti-slavery factions in Congress had attempted to halt the extension of slavery to the new territories obtained from Mexico in the 1846 **Wilmot Proviso**, but these efforts were unsuccessful. The later **Compromise of 1850** admitted the populous California as a free state and Utah and New Mexico to the Union with slavery to be decided by **popular sovereignty**, or by the residents. It also reaffirmed the **Fugitive Slave Act**, which allowed slave owners to pursue escaped slaves to free states and recapture them. It would now be a federal crime to assist escaped slaves, an unacceptable provision to many abolitionists.

Shortly thereafter, Congress passed the **Kansas-Nebraska Act of 1854** which allowed those two territories to decide slavery by popular sovereignty as well, effectively repealing the Missouri Compromise. A new party, the **Republican Party**, was formed by angered Democrats, Whigs, and others as a result; later, one of its members, Abraham Lincoln, would be elected to the presidency. Violence broke out in Kansas between pro- and anti-slavery factions in what became known as **Bleeding Kansas**.

In 1856, an escaped slave, **Dred Scott**, took his case to the Supreme Court to sue for freedom. Scott had escaped to the free state of Illinois and sought to stay there; his former "owner" had argued that he could get him back regardless of the state he was in. The Court heard the case, *Scott v. Sandford*, and ruled in favor of Sandford, upholding the Fugitive Slave Act, the Kansas-Nebraska Act, and nullifying the Missouri Compromise. The Court essentially decreed that African Americans were not entitled to rights under US citizenship.

In 1858, a series of debates between Illinois Senate candidates, Republican **Abraham Lincoln** and Democrat **Stephen Douglas**, showed the deep divides in the nation over slavery and states' rights. During the **Lincoln-Douglas Debates**, Lincoln spoke out against slavery, while Douglas supported the right of states to decide its legality on their own. In 1860, Lincoln was elected to the presidency. Given his outspoken stance against slavery, South Carolina seceded immediately, followed by Mississippi, Alabama, Florida, Louisiana, Georgia, and Texas. They formed the Confederate States of America, or the **Confederacy**, on February 1, 1861, under the leadership of **Jefferson Davis**, a senator from Mississippi.

Shortly after the South's secession, Confederate forces attacked Union troops in Charleston Harbor, South Carolina; the **Battle of Fort Sumter** sparked the Civil War. As a result, Virginia, Tennessee, North Carolina, and Arkansas seceded and joined the Confederacy. West Virginia was formed when the western part of Virginia refused to join the Confederacy.

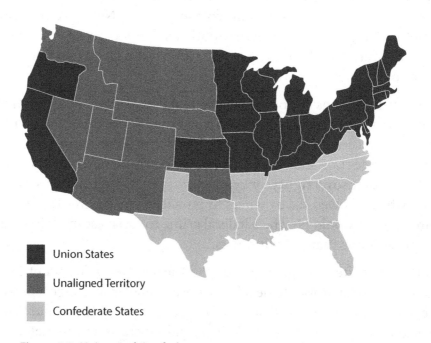

Union States

Unaligned Territory

Confederate States

Figure 1.7. Union and Confederacy

Both sides believed the conflict would be short-lived; however, after the First Battle of Bull Run when the Union failed to rout the Confederacy, it became clear that the war would not end quickly. The Union developed the **Anaconda Plan**, which "squeezed" the Confederacy through a naval blockade and Union control of the Mississippi River. Since the South depended on international trade for much of its income, a naval blockade would have serious economic ramifications.

However, the Second Battle of Bull Run was a tactical Confederate victory, led by **General Robert E. Lee** and Stonewall Jackson. The Union army remained intact, but the loss was a heavy blow to Union morale. The Battle of Antietam was the first battle to be fought on Union soil. Union General George B. McClellan halted General Lee's invasion of Maryland, but failed to defeat Confederate forces. Undaunted, on January 1, 1863, President Lincoln decreed the end of slavery in the rebel states with the **Emancipation Proclamation**. The **Battle of Gettysburg** was a major Union victory. It was the bloodiest battle in American history up to this point; the Confederate army would not recover.

> **DID YOU KNOW?**
>
> President Lincoln later delivered the Gettysburg Address onsite, in which he framed the Civil War as a battle for human rights and equality.

Meanwhile, Union forces led by **General Ulysses S. Grant** gained control over the Mississippi River, completing the Anaconda Plan. The **Battle of Atlanta** was the final major battle of the Civil War, and the Confederacy fell. One of the final conflicts of the war, the Battle of Appomattox Court House, finally resulted in Confederate surrender at Appomattox, Virginia, on April 9, 1865, where General Lee surrendered to General Grant. The war ended shortly after.

Aftermath and Reconstruction

Despite the strong leadership and vast territory of the Confederacy, a larger population, stronger industrial capacity (including weapons-making capacity), the naval blockade of Southern trade, and superior leadership resulted in Union victory. Yet bitterness over Northern victory persisted, and President Lincoln was assassinated on April 15, 1865. Post-war **Reconstruction** would continue without his leadership.

Before his death, Lincoln had crafted the **Ten Percent Plan**: if ten percent of a Southern state's population swore allegiance to the Union, that state would be readmitted. However Lincoln's vice president, Andrew Johnson, enforced Reconstruction weakly and the white supremacist **Ku Klux Klan** emerged to intimidate and kill black people in the South; likewise, states enacted the oppressive **Black Codes** to limit the rights of African Americans.

> **DID YOU KNOW?**
>
> Despite ratifying the amendments, Southern states instituted the Black Codes to continue oppression of freedmen, or freed African Americans, who faced ongoing violence.

As a result, Congress passed the **Civil Rights Act** in 1866, granting citizenship to African Americans and guaranteeing African American men the same rights as white men (later reaffirmed by the Fourteenth Amendment). Eventually former Confederate states also had to ratify the 1865 **Thirteenth Amendment**, which abolished slavery; the **Fourteenth Amendment**, which upheld the provisions of the

Civil Rights Act; and the **Fifteenth Amendment**, which in 1870 granted African American men the right to vote.

Conflict over how harshly to treat the South persisted in Congress and in 1867, a Republican-led Congress passed the **Reconstruction Acts**, placing former Confederate states under the control of the US Army, effectively declaring martial law. Tension and bitterness existed between many Northern authorities and Southern leaders. At the same time, Reconstruction modernized Southern education systems, tax collection, and infrastructure. The **Freedmen's Bureau** was tasked with assisting freed slaves (and poor whites) in the South.

While technically enslaved African Americans had been freed, many slaves were not aware of this; others still remained voluntarily or involuntarily on plantations. All slaves were eventually freed; however, few had education or skills. Despite the Fourteenth Amendment, the rights of African Americans were regularly violated. The **Jim Crow laws** enforced **segregation** in the South.

In 1896, the Supreme Court upheld segregation in *Plessy v. Ferguson* when a mixed-race man, Homer Plessy, was forced off a whites-only train car. When Plessy challenged the law, the Court found that segregation was indeed constitutional, holding that *separate but equal* did still ensure equality under the law. This would remain the law until *Brown v. Board of Education* in 1954.

Black leaders like **Booker T. Washington** and **W.E.B. DuBois** sought solutions. Washington believed in gradual desegregation and vocational education for African Americans, providing it at his **Tuskegee Institute**. DuBois, on the other hand, favored immediate desegregation and believed African Americans should aim for higher education and leadership positions in society. His stance was supported by the advocacy group, the **National Association for the Advancement of Colored People (NAACP)**. These differing views reflected diverse positions within and beyond the African American community over its future. Furthermore, many blacks fled the South for opportunities in the North and West, as part of a greater demographic movement known as the **Great Migration**.

Resentment over the Reconstruction Acts never truly subsided, and military control of the South finally ended with the **Compromise of 1877**, which resolved the disputed presidential election of 1876, granting Rutherford B. Hayes the presidency, and removed troops from the South.

While the Civil War raged and during the chaotic post-war Reconstruction period, settlement of the West continued. California had already grown in population due to the gold rush. In the mid-nineteenth century, **Chinese immigrants** came in large numbers to California, in search of gold but arriving to racial discrimination instead. At the same time, however, the US was opening up trade with East Asia, thanks to **clipper ships** that made journeys across the Pacific Ocean faster and easier. Earlier in 1853, **Commodore Matthew Perry** had used "gunboat diplomacy" to force trade agreements with Japan; even earlier, the United States had signed the **Treaty of Wangxia**, a trade agreement, with Qing Dynasty China.

Unlike Chinese immigrants, Americans of European descent were encouraged to settle the Frontier. The **Homestead Act of 1862** granted 160 acres of land in the West to any settler who promised to settle and work it for a number of years. Frontier life was hard, however, as the land of the Great Plains was difficult to farm. Meanwhile, ranching and herding cattle became popular and profitable. White settlers also hunted the buffalo; mass buffalo killings threatened Native American survival.

Conflict between Native American tribes and white settlers was ongoing. The United States came to an agreement with the Sioux in South Dakota, offering them land as part of the burgeoning **reservation** system. However, by the late nineteenth century, gold was discovered in the Black Hills of South Dakota on the **Great Sioux Reservation**, and the US reneged on its promise. The resulting **Sioux Wars** culminated in the 1876 **Battle of Little Big Horn** and General George Custer's famous "last stand." While the US was defeated in that battle, reinforcements would later defeat the Sioux and the reservation system continued. The spiritual **Ghost Dance Movement** united Plains tribes in the belief that whites would eventually be driven from the land. In 1890, the military forced the Sioux to cease this ritual; the outcome was a massacre at **Wounded Knee** and the death of the Sioux chief, **Sitting Bull**.

In 1887, the **Dawes Act** ended federal recognition of tribes, withdrew tribal land rights, and forced the sale of reservations—tribal land. It also dissolved Native American families. Children were sent to boarding schools, where they were forced to abandon their languages and cultures.

THE GILDED AGE AND THE SECOND INDUSTRIAL REVOLUTION

Back in the Northeast, the market economy and industry were flourishing. Following the war, the **Industrial Revolution** accelerated in the United States. The Industrial Revolution had begun with textile production in Great Britain, fueled in great part by Southern cotton. It evolved in the United States with the development of heavy industry into what would be called the **Second Industrial Revolution**.

The **Gilded Age** saw an era of rapidly growing income inequality, justified by theories like **Social Darwinism** and the **Gospel of Wealth**. These argued that the wealthy had been made rich by God and were more deserving of wealth than others. Much of this wealth was generated by heavy industry in the Second Industrial Revolution (the first being textile driven in Europe). Westward expansion required railroads; railroads required steel, and industrial production required oil: all these commodities spurred the rise of powerful companies like John D. Rockefeller's Standard Oil and Andrew Carnegie's US Steel.

The creation of **monopolies** and **trusts** helped industrial leaders consolidate their control over the entire economy; a small elite grew to hold a huge percentage of income. Monopolies let the same business leaders control the market for their own products. Business leaders in varying industries (monopolies) organized into trusts, ensuring their control over each other's industries, buying and selling from each other, and resulting in the control of the economy by a select few. These processes were made possible thanks to **vertical** and **horizontal integration** of industries. One company would dominate each step in manufacturing a good, from obtaining raw materials to shipping finished product, through vertical integration. Horizontal integration describes the process of companies acquiring their competition, monopolizing their markets. With limited governmental controls or interference in the economy, American **capitalism**—the free market system—was becoming dominated by the elite.

However, the elite were also powering industrial growth. Government corruption led only to weak restrictive legislation like the **Interstate Commerce Act** of 1887, which was to regulate the railroad industry, and the **Sherman Antitrust Act** (1890), which was intended to break up monopolies and trusts, in order to allow for a fairer marketplace; however, these measures would remain largely toothless until President Theodore Roosevelt's "trust-busting" administration in 1901.

Not only were products from the US market economy available in the United States; in order to continue to fuel economic growth, the United States needed more markets abroad. **New Imperialism** described the US approach to nineteenth and early twentieth century imperialism as practiced by the European powers. Rather than controlling territory, the US sought economic connections with countries around the world.

While the free markets and trade of the **capitalist** economy spurred national economic and industrial growth, the **working class**, comprised largely of poor European and Chinese immigrants working in factories and building infrastructure, suffered from dangerous working conditions and other abuses. As the railroads expanded westward, white farmers suffered: they lost their land to corporate interests. In addition, Mexican Americans and Native Americans were harmed and lost land as westward expansion continued with little to no regulations on land use. African Americans in the South, though freed from slavery, were also struggling under **sharecropping**, in which many worked for the same people who had enslaved them, leasing land and equipment at unreasonable rates, essentially trapped in the same conditions they had lived in before.

These harmful consequences led to the development of reform movements, social ideals, and change.

Populism and the Progressive Era

The **People's (Populist) Party** formed in response to corruption and industrialization injurious to farmers (later, it would also support reform in favor of the working class, women, and children). Westward expansion destroyed farmland, pushing small farmers off their land and into debt. Small farmers were also unable to keep up with mechanized farming. Groups like the **National Grange** advocated for farmers. More extreme groups like **Las Gorras Blancas** disrupted the construction of railroads altogether in efforts to protect land from corporate interests.

Farmers were also concerned about fiscal policy. In order to reduce their debt, they believed that a **silver standard** would inflate crop prices by putting more money into national circulation, and formed the **Greenback-Labor Party**. The 1890 **Sherman Silver Purchase Act** allowed Treasury notes to be backed in both gold and silver. However, continuing economic troubles led to the **Panic of 1893**, and the act was repealed.

Meanwhile, the **Colored Farmers' Alliance** formed to support sharecroppers and other African American farmers in the South. Jim Crow laws remained in place in much of the South, reaffirmed by the Supreme Court case *Plessy v. Ferguson*. The NAACP was formed to advocate for African Americans nationwide and still functions today.

At the same time, the **labor movement** emerged to support mistreated industrial workers in urban areas. **Samuel Gompers** led the **American Federation of Labor (AFL)**, using **strikes** and **collective bargaining** to gain protections for industrial workers. The **Knights of Labor** further empowered workers by integrating unskilled workers into actions. The activist **Mother Jones** revolutionized labor by including women, children, and African Americans into labor actions.

Poor conditions led to philosophies of reform. Many workers were inspired by **socialism**, the philosophy developed in Europe that the workers should own the means of production and that wealth should be distributed equally, taking into account strong economic planning. Other radical movements included **utopianism**, whose adherents conceptualized establishing utopian settlements with egalitarian societies. More modern philosophies included the **Social Gospel**, the notion that it was society's obligation to ensure better treatment for workers and immigrants. With the continual rise of the **middle class**, women took a more active role in advocating for the poor and for themselves. Women activists also aligned with labor and the emerging **Progressive Movement**.

With the Progressive **Theodore Roosevelt**'s ascension to the presidency in 1901 following President William McKinley's assassination, the Progressive Era reached its apex. The *trust-buster* Roosevelt enforced the Sherman Antitrust Act and prosecuted the powerful **Northern Securities** railroad monopoly under the Interstate Commerce Act, breaking up trusts and creating a fairer market. He led government involvement in negotiations between unions and industrial powers, culminating in what was known as a *square deal* for fairer treatment of workers. The Progressive Era also saw a series of acts to protect workers, health, farmers, and children under Presidents Roosevelt and Taft.

Roosevelt also continued overseas expansion following McKinley's **Spanish-American War** (1898–1901), in which the US gained control over Spanish territory in the Caribbean, Asia, and the South Pacific.

The Spanish-American War had been the first time the United States had engaged in overseas military occupation and conquest beyond North America, contrary to George Washington's recommendations in his Farewell Address.

During this period, the US annexed Hawaii, Guam, Puerto Rico, and took over the Panama Canal Zone; Cuba became a US protectorate; and the US annexed the Philippines, which would fight an ongoing guerrilla war for independence.

Spanish abuses in Cuba had concerned Americans; however, many events were exaggerated in the media. This sensational **yellow journalism** aroused popular interest in intervention in Cuba. The discovery of a diplomatically embarrassing letter from the Spanish minister de Lôme, along with the mysterious explosion of the battleship USS *Maine* in Havana, spurred the US into action.

Many Americans did not support intervention, however. According to the **Teller Amendment**, Cuba would revert to independence following the war. The US signed a peace treaty with Spain in 1898. As a result, it controlled Puerto Rico and Guam. Despite having promised independence to the Philippines, McKinley elected to keep it; furthermore, under the **Platt Amendment**, the United States effectively took over Cuba despite previous promises.

The **Roosevelt Corollary** to the Monroe Doctrine, which promised US intervention in Latin America in case of European intervention there, essentially gave the US total dominance over Latin America. Under the **Hay-Pauncefote Treaty**, Great Britain relinquished its claims to the Panama Canal Zone to the US. This **new imperialism** expanded US markets and increased US presence and prestige on the global stage.

SAMPLE QUESTIONS

16) **Which of the following is true about the roots of the Civil War?**

   A.   Disagreement over the institution of slavery precipitated the Nullification Crisis, an early example of Southern discontent with the federal government.

   B.   High numbers of immigrants moving to the North in the early nineteenth century represented a threat to the smaller South, which wanted to maintain control over the slaves.

   C.   Lincoln and Douglas provoked anti-slavery sentiment in their debates around the country, bringing attention to a previously uncontested issue.

   D.   The Missouri Compromise, the Compromise of 1850, and the Kansas-Nebraska Act reflected dissent over the future of the country—whether slavery should be extended as the United States grew.

   Answer:

   D.   Correct. These pieces of legislation represent ongoing efforts to bridge the gap between differences in views over slavery in determining the future of the country.

17) How did the Dawes Act impact Native Americans in the West?

   A.   It forced them to move from their ancestral lands to what is today Oklahoma.

   B.   It revoked tribal rights to land and federal recognition of tribes, forcing assimilation.

   C.   It granted them land on reservations: for example, the Sioux received deeds to the Great Sioux Reservation in the Black Hills of South Dakota.

   D.   It provided 160 acres of land to any settler willing to farm land on the Great Plains for at least five years, threatening Native American rights to land.

   Answer:

   B.   Correct. The punitive Dawes Act forced assimilation by revoking federal recognition of tribes, taking lands allotted to tribes and dissolving reservations, and forcing children into assimilationist schools (thereby dividing families).

18) How was a small elite of wealthy businesspersons able to dominate the economy during the Gilded Age?

   A.   The Sherman Antitrust Act put a few expert business leaders in charge of economic policy.

   B.   Monopolies and trusts, developed through horizontal and vertical integration, ensured that the same business leaders controlled the same markets.

   C.   Industrialization was encouraging the United States to shift to a planned economy in keeping with philosophical changes in Europe.

   D.   The silver standard allowed specific businesspeople holding large silver reserves to dominate the market.

   Answer:

   B.   Correct. Horizontal and vertical integration of industries allowed the same companies—and people—to control industries, or create monopolies. Those elites who monopolized specific markets organized trusts so that one group controlled entire sectors of the economy.

19) How did the Spanish-American War change perceptions of the United States?

   A.   It was clear to Europe and Latin America that the United States had military and territorial, in addition to economic, aspirations as an imperial power.

   B.   The United States had begun to prove itself as a military power on the global stage, with strong naval capabilities.

   C.   It was clear that nationalism was strong among the American people.

   D.   all of the above

Answer:

D.   Correct. All of the above answer choices satisfy the question.

20)   **How did the Progressive Movement change the United States during the Second Industrial Revolution?**

A.   Trade unions fought for workers' rights and safety; the Social Gospel, an early philosophy of charity and philanthropy, developed to support the poor and urban disadvantaged.

B.   The Seneca Falls Convention drew attention to the question of women's suffrage.

C.   Progressives argued to extend rights and protections to Native Americans, particularly those displaced by settlement on the Great Plains.

D.   The Supreme Court ruled segregation unconstitutional in *Plessy v. Ferguson.*

Answer:

A.   Correct. Unions improved conditions for industrial workers; the Social Gospel imparted a sense of social responsibility that manifested in laws and regulations protecting the rights and safety of workers, farmers, the poor, and others.

THE UNITED STATES BECOMES A GLOBAL POWER

SOCIOECONOMIC CHANGE AND WORLD WAR I

Social change led by the Progressives in the early twentieth century resulted in better conditions for workers, increased attention toward child labor, and calls for more livable cities.

The Roosevelt administration focused its attention on economic change at the corporate level. The **Sherman Antitrust Act**, despite its intended purpose—to prosecute and dissolve large trusts and create a fairer market place—had actually been used against unions and farmers' alliances. Under Roosevelt, the Act was used to prosecute enormous trusts like the **Northern Securities Company**, which controlled much of the railroad industry, and **Standard Oil**. Actions like this earned Roosevelt his reputation as a trust-buster.

Continuing economic instability also triggered top-down reform. Banks restricting credit and overspeculating on the value of land and interests, coupled with a conservative gold standard, led to the **Panic of 1907**. To stabilize the economy and protect the banking system, Congress passed the **Federal Reserve Act** in 1913. Federal Reserve banks were established to cover twelve regions of the country; commercial banks had to take part in the system, allowing "the Fed" to control interest rates and avoid a similar crisis.

During the Progressive Era, while the United States became increasingly prosperous and stable, Europe was becoming increasingly unstable. Americans were divided over how to respond. Following the Spanish-American War, debate had arisen within the US between **interventionism** and **isolationism**—whether the US should intervene in international matters or not. Interventionists believed in spreading US-style democracy, while isolationists believed in focusing on development at home. This debate became more pronounced with the outbreak of World War I in Europe.

> **DID YOU KNOW?**
>
> Jacob Riis's groundbreaking book and photo essay *How the Other Half Lives* revealed the squalor and poverty the poor urban classes—often impoverished immigrants—endured, leading to more public calls for reform.

Inflammatory events like German **submarine warfare** (U-boats) in the Atlantic Ocean, the sinking of the *Lusitania*, which resulted in many American civilian deaths, the embarrassing **Zimmerman Telegram** (in which Germany promised to help Mexico in an attack on the US), and growing American **nationalism**, or pride in and identification with one's country, triggered US intervention. The US declared war in 1917. With victory in 1918, the US had proven itself a superior military and industrial power. Interventionist **President Woodrow Wilson** played an important role in negotiating the peace; his **Fourteen Points** laid out an idealistic international vision, including an international security organization. However, European powers negotiated and won the harsh **Treaty of Versailles**, which placed the blame for the war entirely on Germany and demanded crippling **reparations** from it, one contributing factor to **World War II** later in the twentieth century. The **League of Nations**, a collective security organization, was formed, but a divided US Congress refused to ratify the Treaty, so the US did not join it. Consequently, the League was weak and largely ineffective.

Divisions between interventionists and isolationists continued. Following the Japanese invasion of Manchuria in 1932, the **Stimson Doctrine** determined US neutrality in Asia. Congress also passed the **Neutrality Acts** of the 1930s in face of conflict in Asia and ongoing tensions in Europe.

Fear of homegrown radicals—particularly communists and anarchists—and xenophobia against immigrants led to the **Red Scare** in 1919 and a series of anti-immigration laws. Congress limited immigration specifically from Asia, Eastern Europe, and Southern Europe with the racist **Emergency Quota Act** of 1921 and **National Origins Act** of 1924.

The ongoing Great Migration of African Americans to the North led to differing views on black empowerment. Leaders like **Marcus Garvey** believed in self-sufficiency for blacks, who were settling in urban areas and facing racial discrimination and isolation. Garvey's **United Negro Improvement Association** would go on to inspire movements like the Black Panthers and the Nation of Islam; however, those radical philosophies of separation were at odds with the NAACP, which believed in integration. Tensions increased with 1919 race riots. In the South, the Ku Klux

Klan was growing in power, and blacks faced intimidation, violence, and death; **lynchings**, in which African Americans were kidnapped and killed, sometimes publicly, occurred frequently.

Despite race riots and discrimination in northern cities, African American culture did flourish and become an integral part of growing American popular culture. The **Harlem Renaissance**, the development and popularity of African American-dominated music (especially **jazz**), literature, and art, was extremely popular nationwide and contributed to the development of American pop culture.

Early technology like radio, motion pictures, and automobiles—products available to the middle class through credit—emerged in the 1920s, changing the US middle class and encouraging a culture of consumption. Furthermore, the women's rights movement was empowered by the heightened visibility of women in the public sphere; the **Nineteenth Amendment**, giving all women the right to vote, was ratified in 1920. However, the **Roaring Twenties**, a seemingly trouble-free period of isolation from chaotic world events, would come to an end.

GREAT DEPRESSION

Following WWI, the United States had experienced an era of consumerism and corruption. The government sponsored **laissez-faire** policies and supported **manufacturing**, flooding markets with cheap consumer goods. Union membership suffered; so did farmers, due to falling crop prices. While mass production helped the emerging middle class afford more consumer goods and improve their living standards, many families resorted to **credit** to fuel consumer spending. These risky consumer loans, **overspeculation** on crops and the value of farmland, and weak banking protections helped bring about the **Great Depression**, commonly dated from October 29, 1929, or *Black Tuesday*, when the stock market collapsed. During the same time period, a major drought occurred in the Great Plains, affecting farmers throughout the region. Millions of Americans faced unemployment and poverty.

Speculation, or margin buying, meant that speculators borrowed money to buy stock, selling it as soon as its price rose. However, since the price of stocks fluctuated, when buyers lost confidence in the market and began selling their shares, the value of stocks fell. Borrowers could not repay their loans; as a result, banks failed.

Following weak responses by the Hoover administration, **Franklin Delano Roosevelt** was elected to the presidency in 1932. FDR offered Americans a *New Deal*: a plan to bring the country out of the Depression. During the *First Hundred Days* of FDR's administration, a series of emergency acts (known as an *alphabet soup* of acts due to their many acronyms) was passed for the immediate repair of the banking system. The **Glass-Steagal Act** established the **Federal Deposit Insurance Corporation (FDIC)** to insure customer deposits in the wake of bank failures. The **Securities and Exchange Commission (SEC)** was established later to monitor stock trading and punish violators of the law. The **Agricultural Adjustment Act (AAA)** subsidized farmers to reduce production, benefitting them by raising the prices of commodities. The **Home Owners Loan Corporation (HOLC)** refinanced mortgages to protect homeowners from losing their homes, and the **Federal Housing Administration (FHA)** was created for the long term to insure low-cost mortgages.

Figure 1.8. Soup Kitchen During the Great Depression

The **Tennessee Valley Authority (TVA)**, was the first large-scale attempt at regional public planning; despite being part of the First Hundred Days, it was a long-term project. While intended to create jobs and bring electricity to the impoverished, rural inhabitants of the Tennessee Valley area, one of its true objectives was to accurately measure the cost of electric power, which had been supplied by private companies. The TVA was the first public power company and still operates today.

FDR did not only address economic issues; a number of acts provided relief to the poor and unemployed. The federal government allotted aid to states to be distributed directly to the poor through the **Federal Emergency Relief Act**. The federal government distributed funding to states through the **Public Works Administration (PWA)** for the purpose of developing infrastructure and to provide construction jobs for the unemployed. Likewise, the **Civilian Conservation Corps (CCC)** offered employment in environmental conservation and management projects. Later, during the **Second New Deal**, the **Works Progress Administration (WPA)** was established. The WPA was a long-term project that generated construction jobs on national infrastructure projects. It also employed writers and artists through the **Federal Writers' Project** and the **Federal Art Project**.

The New Deal addressed labor issues as well. The **Wagner Act** ensured the right to unionize and established the **National Labor Relations Board (NLRB)**. Strengthening unions guaranteed collective bargaining rights and protected workers.

FDR was a Democrat in the Progressive tradition; the Progressive legacy of social improvement was apparent throughout the New Deal and his administration. The New Deal and its positive impact on the poor, the working class, unions, and immigrants led these groups to support the Democratic Party.

INTERNATIONAL AFFAIRS AND WORLD WAR II

The entire world suffered from the Great Depression, and Europe became increasingly unstable. With the rise of the extremist Nazi Party in Germany, the Nazi leader Adolf Hitler led German takeovers of several European countries and threatened US allies, bombing Britain. However, the United States, weakened by the Great Depression and bound by the Neutrality Acts, remained militarily uncommitted in the war. However, the Neutrality Act of 1939 allowed cash-and-carry arms sales to combat participants; in this way, the United States could support its allies (namely, Great Britain).

FDR was increasingly concerned about the rise of fascism in Europe, seeing it as a global threat. To ally with and support Great Britain without technically declaring war on Germany, FDR convinced Congress to enact the **Lend-Lease Act**, directly supplying Britain with military aid, in place of cash-and-carry. In response to the nonaggression pact signed by Hitler and Stalin, FDR and the British Prime Minister **Winston Churchill** signed the **Atlantic Charter**, which laid out the anti-fascist agenda of free trade and self-determination. To garner domestic support, FDR spoke publicly about the **Four Freedoms**: freedom of speech, freedom of religion, freedom from want, and freedom from fear.

However, after the Japanese attack on **Pearl Harbor** on December 7, 1941, the US entered the war. Despite being attacked by Japan (a German ally), the United States focused first on the European theater. The Allied powers—the US, Great Britain, and the Soviet Union—agreed that Hitler was the primary global threat. The United States focused on eliminating the Nazi threat in the air and at sea, destroying Nazi U-boats (submarines) in the Atlantic. The US also engaged Germany in North Africa, defeating its troops to approach fascist Italy from the Mediterranean. On June 6, 1944, or **D-Day**, the US led the invasion of German-controlled Europe at Normandy. After months of fighting, following the exhausting **Battle of the Bulge** when the Allies faced fierce German resistance, the Allies entered Germany and ended the war in Europe.

The United States was then able to focus more effectively on the war in the Pacific. The United States had broken Japanese code, yet the **Navajo Code Talkers**, using the Navajo language, made it impossible for Japan to crack US code. The US strategy of **island hopping** allowed it to take control of Japanese-held Pacific islands, proceeding closer to Japan itself despite **kamikaze** attacks on US ships, in which Japanese fighter pilots intentionally crashed their planes into US ships. President **Harry Truman** had taken power following FDR's death in 1945. Rather than force a US invasion of Japan, which would have resulted in massive casualties, he authorized the bombing of **Hiroshima** and **Nagasaki** in Japan, the only times that **nuclear weapons** have been used in conflict. The war ended with Japanese surrender on September 2, 1945.

The **United Nations** was formed in the wake of the Second World War, modeled after the failed League of Nations. Unlike the League, however, it included a **Security Council** of major world powers, which could intervene militarily in unstable global situations. With most of Europe destroyed, the US and the Soviet Union emerged as the two global **superpowers**.

In 1945, Stalin, Churchill, and Roosevelt had met at the **Yalta Conference** to determine the future of Europe. The Allies had agreed on free elections in European countries. However, following the war the USSR occupied Eastern Europe, preventing free elections. The United States saw this as a betrayal of the agreement at Yalta. Furthermore, while the US-led **Marshall Plan** began rebuilding Europe, the USSR consolidated its presence and power in Eastern European countries, forcing them to reject Marshall aid. This division would destroy the alliance between the Soviets and the West, leading to the **Cold War** between the two superpowers and the emergence of a **bipolar world**.

> **DID YOU KNOW?**
>
> Japanese-Americans faced discrimination at home due to their ethnicity. Forced into internment camps, Japanese-Americans challenged this violation of their rights in *Korematsu v. US*; however, the Supreme Court ruled in favor of the government.

COLD WAR AT HOME AND ABROAD

With the collapse of the relationship between the USSR and the US, fear of **communism** grew. Accusations of communist sympathies against public figures ran rampant during the **McCarthy era** in the 1950s, reflecting domestic anxieties.

The **Truman Doctrine** stated that the US would support any country threatened by authoritarianism (communism). This policy lead to the **Korean War** (1950 – 1953), a conflict between the US and Soviet- and Chinese-backed North Korean forces, which ended in a stalemate. The policy of **containment**, to contain Soviet (communist) expansion, defined US foreign policy. According to **domino theory**, once one country fell to communism, others would quickly follow. Other incidents included the **Bay of Pigs** invasion in Cuba (1961), a failed effort to topple the communist government of Fidel Castro, and the **Cuban Missile Crisis** (1962), when Soviet missiles were discovered in Cuba and military crisis was narrowly averted, both under the administration of the popular President **John F. Kennedy**.

Meanwhile, in Southeast Asia, communist forces in North Vietnam were gaining power. Congress never formally declared war in Vietnam but gave the president authority to intervene militarily there through the **Gulf of Tonkin Resolution** (1964). However, this protracted conflict—the **Vietnam War**—also led to widespread domestic social unrest, which only increased with US deaths there, especially after the Vietnamese **Tet Offensive** (1968). The US ultimately withdrew from Vietnam. North Vietnamese forces, led by **Ho Chi Minh**, took over the entire country.

SAMPLE QUESTIONS

21) **Which of the following precipitated US entry into the First World War?**

    A. the sinking of the *Lusitania*

    B. nationalism stirred up by the Zimmerman telegram

    C. the threat of German U-boats in the Atlantic

    D. all of the above

    Answer:

    D. Correct. All of the above events together precipitated US entry into the First World War.

22) **How did the United States change in the 1920s?**

    A. The Great Migration ceased.

    B. African American culture became increasingly influential.

    C. The Great Depression caused high unemployment.

    D. Thanks to the New Deal, millions of Americans found jobs.

    Answer:

    B. Correct. The Harlem Renaissance is one example of the emergence of African American culture in the public sphere; as US popular culture developed, African American contributions influenced it.

23) **What was the purpose of the United Nations Security Council?**

    A. to provide a means for international military intervention in case of conflict that could threaten global safety, in order to avoid another world war

    B. to provide a forum for the superpowers to maintain a dialogue

    C. to provide a means for countries to counter the power of the US and USSR in an effort to limit the reach of the superpowers

    D. to develop a plan to rebuild Europe and Japan

Answer:

A.   **Correct.** The Security Council was (and is) able to militarily intervene in cases of armed conflict that could pose a global threat.

24) **How did the New Deal repair the damage of the Great Depression and help the United States rebuild?**

A.   Immediate economic reforms stabilized the economy during the First Hundred Days; later, longer-term public works programs provided jobs to relieve unemployment and develop infrastructure.

B.   Social programs initiated during the First Hundred Days provided jobs for Americans; measures to protect homeowners, landholders, and bank deposits followed to guarantee financial security.

C.   Programs like the Tennessee Valley Authority helped the government determine proper pricing and institute price controls for important public goods.

D.   FDR proposed supporting banks and big business with federal money in order to reinvigorate the market by limiting government intervention.

Answer:

A.   **Correct.** FDR focused on immediate economic stabilization upon taking office, then attacked poverty and unemployment on a sustainable basis.

25) **Why did the former allies, the United States and the Soviet Union, turn against each other following the end of the Second World War?**

A.   Stalin felt that the Marshall Plan should have been extended to the Soviet Union.

B.   Because of the fear of communism in the United States, the US had considered invading the USSR following the occupation of Nazi Germany.

C.   Despite assurances to the contrary, the USSR occupied Eastern European countries, preventing free elections in those countries.

D.   The Soviet Union was concerned that the United States would use the nuclear bomb again.

Answer:

C.   **Correct.** Stalin's refusal to permit free elections in the countries of Eastern Europe was considered a betrayal of the agreement reached at Yalta, and a major reason for the collapse of the US-Soviet relationship.

Postwar and Contemporary United States

Civil Rights and Social Change

During the 1960s, the US experienced social and political change, starting with the election of the young and charismatic John F. Kennedy to the presidency. Later, President **Lyndon B. Johnson**'s administration saw the passage of liberal legislation in support of the poor and of civil rights. The **Civil Rights Movement**, led by activists like the **Rev. Dr. Martin Luther King, Jr.** and **Malcolm X**, fought for African American rights in the South, including the abolition of segregation, and also for better living standards for Blacks in northern cities.

Civil rights came to the forefront with the 1954 Supreme Court case *Brown v. Board of Education*, when the Warren Court (so-called after Chief Justice Earl Warren) found segregation unconstitutional, overturning its decision in *Plessy v. Ferguson*. *Brown* took place shortly after the desegregation of the armed forces, and public support for civil rights and racial equality was growing.

The **Southern Christian Leadership Conference (SCLC)** and Dr. King believed in civil disobedience, non-violent protest. In Montgomery, Alabama, **Rosa Parks**, an African American woman, was arrested for refusing to give up her seat to a white man on a bus. Buses were segregated at the time, and leaders including Dr. King organized the successful **Montgomery Bus Boycott** to challenge segregation. Building on their success, civil rights activists, now including the **Student Nonviolent Coordinating Committee (SNCC)**, led peaceful protests, sit-ins, and boycotts against segregation at lunch counters, in stores, at public pools, and other public places.

The movement grew to include voter registration campaigns that included students and other activists (both black and white) from around the country—the **Freedom Riders**, so-called because they rode buses from around the country to join the movement in the South. The movement gained visibility as non-violent protesters at government and public facilities and on university campuses faced violence from the police and state authorities, including attacks by water cannons and police dogs.

The Civil Rights Movement became a major national issue. Civil rights workers organized the **March on Washington** in 1963, when Dr. King delivered his famous *I Have a Dream* speech. Widespread public support for civil rights legislation was impossible for the government to ignore. In 1964, Congress passed the **Civil Rights Act**, which outlawed segregation.

However, African Americans' voting rights were still not sufficiently protected. According to the Fifteenth and Nineteenth Amendments, all African Americans—men and women—had the right to vote, but many Southern states restricted voting with literacy tests and poll taxes, which disproportionately affected African Americans. Dr. King and civil rights workers organized a march from Selma to Montgomery, Alabama, to draw attention to this issue; however it ended in violence as marchers were attacked by police. In 1965, led by President Lyndon B. Johnson, Congress passed the **Voting Rights Act**, which forbade restrictions impeding the ability of African Americans to vote, including literacy tests. Separately, the **Twenty-Fourth Amendment** made poll taxes unconstitutional.

Figure 1.9. March on Washington

Meanwhile, **Malcolm X** was an outspoken proponent of **black empowerment**, particularly for African Americans in urban areas. Unlike Martin Luther King, Jr., who believed in integration, Malcolm X and other activists, including groups like the **Black Panthers**, believed that African Americans should focus on strengthening their own communities rather than advocating for integration and legislative change.

The Civil Rights Movement extended beyond the Deep South. **Cesar Chavez** founded the **United Farm Workers (UFW)**, which organized Hispanic and migrant farm workers in California and the Southwest to advocate for unionizing and collective bargaining. Farm workers were underpaid and faced racial discrimination. The UFW used boycotts and non-violent tactics similar to those used by civil rights activists in the South; Cesar Chavez also used hunger strikes to raise awareness of the problems faced by farm workers.

DID YOU KNOW?

Today, some states have instituted voter identification laws similar to literacy tests and poll taxes, which disproportionately affect minorities.

The Civil Rights Movement also included **feminist** activists who fought for fairer treatment of women in the workplace and for women's reproductive rights. The **National Organization for Women** and feminist leaders like **Gloria Steinem** led the movement for equal pay for women in the workplace. The landmark case of *Roe v. Wade* struck down federal restrictions on abortion.

The **American Indian Movement (AIM)** brought attention to injustices and discrimination suffered by Native Americans nationwide. Ultimately it was able to achieve more tribal autonomy and address problems facing Native American communities throughout the United States.

In New York City in 1969, the **Stonewall riots** occurred in response to police repression of the gay community. These riots and subsequent organized activism are considered the beginning of the LGBT rights movement.

Johnson launched a **War on Poverty**, passing reform legislation to support the poor. The **Medicare Act** provided medical care to elderly Americans; the creation of the **Department of Housing and Urban Development** increased the federal role in housing and urban issues. Johnson's **Head Start** program provisded early intervention for disadvantaged children before elementary school (and still does today); the **Elementary and Secondary Education Act** increased funding for primary and secondary education. Additionally, the **Immigration Act of 1965** overturned the provisions of the Emergency Quota Act, ending the racist limitations on immigrants to the US.

At the same time, LBJ's overseas agenda was increasingly unpopular. Adhering to containment and domino theory, Johnson drew the United States deeper into conflict in Southeast Asia. The **Vietnam War** was extremely unpopular in the US due to high casualties, the draft (mandatory military service for young men) and what seemed to many to be the purposelessness of the war. Student activists engaged in widespread protest. The emergence of a youth **counterculture** added to a sense of rebellion among Americans, usurping government authority and challenging traditional values.

The Rise of Conservatism

Radical social change in the 1960s, coupled with the toll of the Vietnam War on the American public, led to backlash against liberalism. Social and political **conservatism** arose as a response to the increased role of government in public life, high rates of government spending, and challenges to traditional social norms. The conservative **Richard Nixon** became president in 1970.

During Nixon's administration, the conflict in Vietnam ended and a diplomatic relationship with China began. Nixon also oversaw economic reforms—he lifted the gold standard in an effort to stop **stagflation**, a phenomenon when both unemployment and inflation are high at the same time. Ending the gold standard reduced the value of the dollar in relation to other global currencies, and foreign investment in the United States increased. However, the Nixon administration also suffered from corruption. A burglary at the Democratic National Headquarters, based at the Watergate Hotel, was connected to the Oval Office. The **Watergate scandal** eventually forced Nixon to resign, further destroying many Americans' faith in their government.

During the 1970s, the economy suffered due to US involvement in the Middle East. US support for Israel in the Six Day War and 1973 Yom Kippur War caused the Arab-dominated **OPEC** (the Organization of Petroleum Exporting Countries) to boycott the US. As a result, oil prices skyrocketed. In the 1979 Iranian Revolution and **hostage crisis**, when staff at the US embassy in Tehran were taken hostage by anti-American activists, the economy suffered from another oil shock. While President Jimmy Carter had been able to negotiate peace between Israel and Egypt in the **Camp David Accords**, he was widely perceived as ineffective. Carter lost the presidency in 1980 to the conservative Republican **Ronald Reagan**.

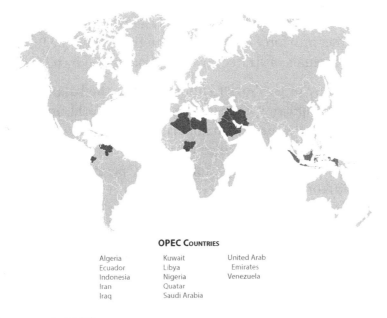

OPEC Countries

Algeria	Kuwait	United Arab
Ecuador	Libya	Emirates
Indonesia	Nigeria	Venezuela
Iran	Quatar	
Iraq	Saudi Arabia	

Figure 1.10. OPEC

Reagan championed domestic tax cuts and an aggressive foreign policy against the Soviet Union. The Reagan Revolution revamped the economic system, cutting taxes and government spending. According to supply-side economics (popularly known as *Reaganomics* or *trickle-down economics*), cutting taxes on the wealthy and providing investment incentives would cause wealth to "trickle down" to the middle and working classes and the poor. However, tax cuts forced Congress to cut or eliminate social programs that benefitted millions of those same Americans. Later, the **Tax Reform Act** of 1986 ended progressive income taxation.

Despite promises to lower government spending, the Reagan administration invested heavily in the military in an **arms race** with the Soviet Union. The Reagan administration also funded advanced military technology to intimidate the Soviets, despite having signed the **Strategic Arms Limitation Treaties (SALT I and II)** limiting nuclear weapons and other strategic armaments in the 1970s. Ultimately, the US would outspend the USSR militarily, a precipitating factor in the fall of the USSR.

Conservative values became publicly popular. Since the Civil Rights Movement, many Southern Democrats switched loyalties to the Republican Party. At the same time, the Democrats gained the support of African Americans and other minority groups who benefitted from civil rights and liberal legislation. During the Reagan era, conservative Republicans espoused a return to "traditional" values. **Christian fundamentalism** became popular, particularly among white conservatives. Groups like **Focus on the Family** lobbied against civil rights reform for women and advocated for traditional, two-parent, heterosexual families.

THE END OF THE COLD WAR AND GLOBALIZATION

The administration of **George H. W. Bush** signed the Strategic Arms Reduction Treaty (**START**) with the Soviet Union in 1991, shortly before the dissolution of the USSR. It would enter into force in 1994 between the US and the Russian Federation to limit the large arsenals of strategic weapons possessed by both countries.

With the collapse of the Soviet Union in 1991, the balance of international power changed. The bipolar world became a unipolar world, and the United States was the sole superpower. The first major crisis occurred in the Middle East when Iraq, led by **Saddam Hussein**, invaded oil-rich Kuwait. The US intervened, with international support. The resulting **Gulf War**, or **Operation Desert Storm** (1991)—cemented the status of the US as the world's sole superpower; Saddam's forces were driven from Kuwait, and Iraq was restrained by sanctions and no-fly zones.

With the election of President **Bill Clinton** in 1992, the US took an active international role, helping broker peace deals in the former Yugoslavia, Northern Ireland, and the Middle East. Clinton's election also indicated a more liberal era in American society: while conservative elements remained, changing attitudes toward minorities in the public sphere and increased global communication (especially with the advent of the internet) were a hallmark of the 1990s.

As part of **globalization**, the facilitation of global commerce and communication, the Clinton administration prioritized free trade. The United States signed the **North American Free Trade Agreement (NAFTA)** with Mexico and Canada, removing trade restrictions throughout North America. The Clinton administration also eased financial restrictions in the United States. These changes were controversial: many American jobs went overseas, especially manufacturing jobs, where labor was cheaper. Furthermore, globalization facilitated the movement of people. **Immigration reform** would be a major issue into the twenty-first century.

Clinton faced dissent in the mid-1990s with a conservative resurgence. A movement of young conservatives elected to Congress in 1994 promised a **Contract with America**, a conservative platform promising a return to lower taxes and traditional values. Clinton also came under fire for personal scandals. Despite these controversies and political division, society became increasingly liberal. Technology like the **internet** facilitated national and global communication, media, and business; minority groups like the LGBT community engaged in more advocacy; and environmental issues became more important to the public.

The Twenty-First Century

By the end of the twentieth century, the United States had established itself as the dominant global economic, military, and political power. The US dominated global trade: American corporations established themselves globally, taking advantage of free trade to exploit cheap labor pools and less restrictive manufacturing environments (at the expense of American workers). American culture was widely popular: since the early twentieth century, American pop culture like music, movies, television shows, and fashion was enjoyed worldwide.

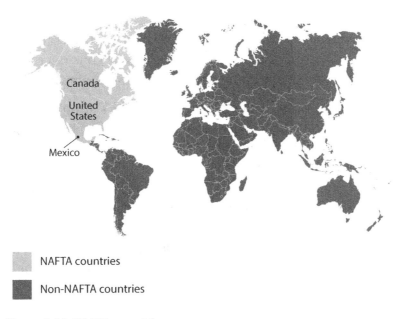

Figure 1.11. NAFTA countries

However, globalization also facilitated global conflict. The United States had been relatively untouched by large-scale terrorist attacks. That changed on **September 11, 2001**, when the terrorist group **al Qaeda** hijacked airplanes, attacking New York and Washington, DC, in the largest attack on US soil since the Japanese bombing of Pearl Harbor. The 9/11 attacks triggered an aggressive military and foreign policy under the administration of President **George W. Bush**, who declared a *War on Terror*, an open-ended global conflict against terror organizations and their supporters.

Following the attacks, the US struck suspected al Qaeda bases in Afghanistan, beginning the **Afghanistan War**, during which time the US occupied the country. Suspected terrorist fighters captured there and elsewhere during the War on Terror were held in a prison in **Guantanamo Bay**, Cuba, which was controversial because it did not initially offer any protections afforded to prisoners of war under the Geneva Conventions.

President Bush believed in the doctrine of **preemption**, that if the US was aware of a threat, it should preemptively attack the source of that threat. In 2003, the US attacked Iraq, believing that Iraq held **weapons of mass destruction** that could threaten the United States. This assumption was later revealed to be false; however, the **Iraq War** deposed Saddam Hussein and led to a long-term occupation of the country as well as destabilization and violence in Iraq.

At home, Congress passed the **USA Patriot Act** to respond to fears of more terrorist attacks on US soil; this legislation gave the federal government unprecedented—and, some argued, unconstitutional—powers of surveillance over the American public.

Despite the tense climate, social liberalization continued in the US. Following the Bush administration, during which tax cuts and heavy reliance on credit helped push the country into the **Great Recession**, the first African American president, **Barack Obama**, was elected in 2008. Under his presidency, the US emerged from the recession, ended its occupations of Iraq and Afghanistan, passed the Affordable Care Act, which reformed the healthcare system, and legalized same-sex marriage. The Obama administration also oversaw the passage of consumer protection acts, increased support for students, and safety nets for homeowners.

In 2016, the celebrity real estate developer **Donald Trump** won the presidency in an intensely contested election against **Hillary Clinton**, former senator, Obama's secretary of state, and the first female Democratic nominee for president. Economic malaise, racial tensions, urbanization, and other issues are thought to be contributing to national division. Some strongly support Trump, whose isolationist policies include withdrawing from the international Paris Agreement to combat climate change, banning citizens of some Muslim-majority countries from the US, and cutting involvement in NATO. Others vehemently disagree with his positions, accuse him of corruption, and are suspicious of the authenticity of his election, fearing it was unfairly influenced by the Russian Federation.

SAMPLE QUESTIONS

26) Why did the Civil Rights Movement continue to push for legislative change even after the passage of the 1964 Civil Rights Act?

   A.   While the Civil Rights Act provided legal protections to African Americans and other groups, many believed it did not go far enough as it did not outlaw segregation.

   B.   Leaders like Malcolm X believed further legislative reform would ensure better living conditions for blacks in cities.

   C.   Civil rights leaders wanted legislation to punish white authorities in the South that had oppressed African Americans.

   D.   Legal restrictions like literacy tests, poll taxes, and voter registration issues inhibited African Americans from exercising their right to vote, especially in the South.

   Answer:

   D.   Correct. Despite the end to legal segregation, discrimination was deeply entrenched, and laws still existed to prevent African Americans from voting. Civil rights activists worked to ensure the passage of the Voting Rights Act in 1965.

27) Which of the following best describes liberalism under LBJ?

   A.   Liberalism was the philosophy that the government should be deeply involved in improving society at home, and work on fighting communism abroad.

   B.   According to liberalism, the US should devote its resources to improving life at home for the disadvantaged, but refrain from direct intervention in international conflict.

   C.   Liberals believed in moderate social programs, but that spending should be limited.

   D.   Liberalism frowns upon conflict intervention, as shown by the mass demonstrations against the Vietnam War in the 1960s.

   Answer:

   A.   Correct. LBJ believed in forming a Great Society and launched government programs to support the disadvantaged; he also waged an unsuccessful war against communism in Southeast Asia.

28) Which of the following best describes globalization?

   A.   the free movement of goods and services across borders

   B.   easier communication worldwide thanks to technology like the internet

   C.   facilitated movement of persons from one country to another

   D.   all of the above

Answer:

D.   Correct. Globalization is a multifaceted phenomenon that takes into account all the factors listed above.

29) **How did Reagan's economic policies affect working class and poor Americans?**

A.   They had little effect on these classes because the United States has a free market economy.

B.   They increased taxes by eliminating the progressive income tax and cut social programs needed by many disadvantaged people.

C.   They benefitted the working and middle classes by cutting taxes and increasing investment opportunities.

D.   Despite Reagan's tax cuts, the government was able to fund all social programs, so lower income Americans who used them were unaffected by changes in revenue.

Answer:

B.   Correct. Low taxes on the wealthy were thought to encourage investment in the economy; as a result, wealth would "trickle down" to other Americans. In practice, lower taxes meant less government revenue, and many social programs were cut.

30) **Which best describes the Bush doctrine of preemption?**

A.   The US believed that in order to contain terrorism, it had to occupy countries that might harbor terrorists.

B.   Fearing that the entire Middle East would succumb to terrorists, the Bush administration established a presence in the centrally located country of Iraq to avoid a "domino effect" of regime collapse.

C.   The Bush administration justified international intervention and foreign invasion without previous provocation in order to preempt possible terrorist attacks.

D.   The US held prisoners captured during the War on Terror at Guantanamo Bay, where they were not treated as prisoners of war under the Geneva Conventions.

Answer:

C.   Correct. Preemption was used to justify the 2003 invasion of Iraq, on the assumption that Iraq had weapons of mass destruction it intended to use or to provide for terrorist attacks against the United States.

Practice Test

WORLD HISTORY PRE-1450 (30)

1

The Hittites were able to expand from Anatolia due to

A.   superior seafaring technology, allowing expansion into the Mediterranean.

B.   superior military technology, including chariots and weaponry.

C.   advanced technology imported from Greece.

D.   their development of bronze metallurgy.

2

During the Peloponnesian War,

A.   the dominant Hellenic powers, Crete and Sparta, went to war with each other.

B.   the dominant Hellenic powers, Athens and Sparta, went to war with the Ionian Greeks in Anatolia.

C.   Greece was able to unite as the dominant powers, Athens and Sparta, fought against Persia and the Ionian Greeks.

D.   the dominant Hellenic powers, Athens and Sparta, went to war with each other.

3

How did the Neolithic Era mark a major development in human evolution?

A.   the development of agriculture and beginning of settled societies

B.   the early use of the wheel

C.   the use of bronze to develop basic tools

D.   early medical treatment

4

During the Paleolithic Era,

A.   *Homo sapiens* was the only species of human in existence.

B.   multiple species of human existed.

C.   *Homo sapiens* likely eliminated all competition for resources.

D.   hominids had not yet evolved.

5

During the Neolithic Era,

A.   *Homo sapiens* was the only species of human in existence.

B.   multiple species of human existed.

C.   *Homo sapiens* likely eliminated all competition for resources.

D.   humans had not yet evolved.

6

There is evidence that the Bronze Age

A.   was a purely European phenomenon.

B.   only occurred in the Fertile Crescent.

C.   can be attributed to widespread sources of early bronze metallurgy.

D.   was a Chinese development.

7

Which of the following best describes the caste system in India?

A.   It is a defined, unchangeable social and religious hierarchy, determined by birth.

B.   It is a changeable social hierarchy.

C.   It is a hierarchy determined by skills and education wherein one's position can be changed.

D.   It is a defined, unchangeable social hierarchy, determined by birth.

8

What concept(s) did early Chinese imperial civilization and early Fertile Crescent civilizations share?

A.   centralized government structure

B.   written language

C.   monotheism

D.   A and B only

9

Which of the following statements best explains the relevance of bronze metallurgy in early human civilizations?

A.   Bronze technology allowed early societies in the Fertile Crescent to develop improved irrigation.

B.   The Bronze Age gave rise to the Neolithic Era.

C.   The development of bronze allowed humans to create copper.

D.   Early civilizations like the Sumerians were able to use bronze for tools and weapons; geographic expansion and technological innovation (including in weaponry) resulted.

10

The Qin dynasty was able to consolidate its power in China due to which of the following?

A.   The Qin enforced Confucianism throughout China as a means to consolidate its power.

B.   The Qin developed a common written language, allowing them to unite the disparate Chinese-speaking groups of people throughout China.

C.   Emerging dominant following the Warring States period, the Qin developed standardized weights and measures and a unified bureaucracy.

D.   All of the above are correct.

11

What development under the Shang dynasty contributed to Chinese unity?

A.   early writing, which helped united disparate Chinese-speaking peoples across a wide landscape

B.   the concept of the Mandate of Heaven, which taught that the emperor was chosen by a divine source to rule, helping consolidate his power

C.   the construction of the Forbidden City, which strengthened the power of the emperor and further centralized it

D.   all of the above

12

The Babylonians are known for having developed an early form of

A.   irrigation, increasing agricultural production in the fertile areas near the Tigris and Euphrates Rivers.

B.   cuneiform, the first known example of writing in which characters were connected to form words.

C.   rule of law: the Code of Hammurabi.

D.   iron weaponry and chariots, enabling them to control large areas of land.

13

How would society develop in the civilizations of the Indus Valley region?

A.   A society based on respect for wisdom and harmony became entrenched in the region.

B.   A hierarchical caste system intertwined with religion came to delineate social roles and status.

C.   The teachings of Siddhartha Gautama would become popular and persist in the region until the present day.

D.   A strict social system of exams would be established, creating a hierarchy of educated government officials.

14

Buddhism is practiced

A.   in parts of the Himalayas, East and Southeast Asia.

B.   widely throughout India and the Himalayas.

C.   only in Tibet.

D.   only in Southeast Asia.

15

Despite the period of relative stability enjoyed by Europe during the High Middle Ages, the Black Death resulted in which of the following outcomes?

A.   European powers were made vulnerable to attacks by the Magyars, who toppled the disorganized Holy Roman Empire.

B.   Instability in Europe led to military conflict, division within the Catholic Church, and weakening of the Holy Roman Empire.

C.   The Mongols were able to expand their empire into Eastern Europe.

D.   Islamic powers were able to completely conquer the Iberian Peninsula as a result of instability there.

16

Following the collapse of the Western Roman Empire and the subsequent, disorganized "Dark Ages" in Europe,

A.   The Catholic Church based in Rome lost power in Western Europe to the rising Greek Orthodox Church based in Constantinople.

B.   The Byzantine Empire was able to conquer unorganized European land in what is today Germany.

C.   Charlemagne united parts of Western and Central Europe—what would become the Holy Roman Empire—leading to a period of stability.

D.   Charlemagne united parts of Western and Central Europe (including what would become France) under his rule, leading to a period of stability.

17

Many scholars argue that modern banking began in Venice in the fifteenth century. Which of the following strengthens this argument?

A.   Venice was the first major colonial power, developing mercantilism.

B.   Venice was a center of intellectual and cultural development.

C.   Venice was a commercial center, ideally situated to profit from goods imported on the Silk Road and from Africa.

D.   Venice was not badly affected by the plague.

18

Judaism developed in which of the following areas?

A.   Egypt

B.   the Levant

C.   Mesopotamia

D.   the Fertile Crescent

19

In feudal Europe, serfs were

A.   enslaved by the lords and knights.

B.   bonded to the land but under the protection of the lords.

C.   forced to fight for the lords.

D.   able to eventually purchase their freedom from the knights in exchange for support fighting.

20

Which of the following is the main reason for the development of the Sunni-Shi'a schism in early Islam?

A.   Sunnis believed that early Muslims should conquer lands west of the Arabian Peninsula, while Shi'ites thought it would make more sense strategically to invade the Mesopotamian regions and Persia.

B.   Sunnis prioritized military conquest over Muhammad's religious and philosophical teachings, a development with which Shi'ites vehemently disagreed.

C.   Sunnis were more willing to accept Jews and Christians as "People of the Book," but Shi'ites felt that they should be converted to Islam, or forced out of communities controlled by Muslims.

D.   Sunnis and Shi'ites disagreed over the appropriate line of succession following the death of the Prophet Muhammad.

21

While the Crusades enriched Europe in many ways, they did not

A. provide new learning to the West.

B. result in lasting land gains.

C. provide religious indulgences.

D. offer the opportunity to gain personal wealth.

22

How was Russia affected by the schism between Byzantine (Greek Orthodox) Christianity and the Roman Catholic Church?

A. Russia was unaffected.

B. Strong papal influences within Europe extended into Kiev and Russia, and Vladimir I converted to Catholicism, encouraging his subjects to do the same.

C. Byzantine missionaries moved north into Kiev and Russian territories; as a result, Vladimir I converted to Greek Orthodox Christianity and had his subjects do the same.

D. Disagreeing with the Catholic Church, Russia developed Eastern Orthodox Christianity and a separate Russian church.

23

The collapse of the Mongol Empire was due in part to which of the following developments?

I. the rise of Islam and the growing power of the Abbasid Caliphate

II. Ivan the Great's consolidation of power and conquest of Moscow

III. the overthrow of the Yuan dynasty by the Ming dynasty in China

A. I, II, and III

B. I and II only

C. II and III only

D. I and III only

24

One reason Charlemagne was able to retain legitimacy and hold power in an unstable Europe was because

A. He was crowned by the pope and had the support of the Catholic Church.

B. He had the support of the serfs, having pledged to end the feudal system.

C. He encouraged knights to travel to the Middle East to fight the Crusades.

D. He was seen as a counter to the tremendous power of the Catholic Church.

25

As head of the Catholic Church, the pope was particularly influential because

A. Catholicism had more followers than Greek Orthodox Christianity.

B. the pope held not only spiritual power, but also political power.

C. the church had special influence in Europe because it was based in Rome, a city of historical significance.

D. the pope had direct political control over most lords throughout feudal Europe.

26

Europeans were encouraged to fight in the Crusades for which of the following reasons?

A. They were promised indulgences by the pope—forgiveness for any sins committed in the Crusades.

B. They were encouraged to keep wealth they might gain in the Middle East.

C. They were encouraged to fight against perceived threats to Christianity in the Middle East.

D. all of the above

27

Following the defeat of the Mongol-backed Yuan dynasty, the powerful Ming dynasty demonstrated its imperial strength in which of the following ways?

A. expanding military occupation through Central Asia into Mongol-held territories in Russia

B. consolidating and projecting imperial power by building the Great Wall

C. accepting tribute from Muslim powers along the Silk Road to strengthen Chinese influence in Central Asia

D. developing a strong navy to expand its global exploratory capabilities as a counter to Portuguese naval exploration

28

The Kingdom of Mali developed due to

A. its control over the trans-Saharan trade routes, enabling it to tax traders transporting goods between Morocco and the Atlantic coast.

B. its ability to repel Islamic influences from the north.

C. its control over gold and salt resources, generating tremendous wealth for the kingdom.

D. its control over the trans-Saharan slave trade.

29

Despite never making significant land gains in the Levant, Europe benefitted from the Crusades through which of the following ways?

A.   Many knights returned from the Middle East with Middle Eastern, Muslim wives, bringing religious and ethnic diversity to Europe.

B.   Crusaders returned to Europe with new language skills, helping reinvigorate trade on the Silk Road through Asia and Muslim-held lands into China.

C.   Crusaders returned to Europe with knowledge of Arab-Islamic technology, navigation, and science, contributing to European learning and seafaring capability; this knowledge would eventually contribute to the colonial era and the Scientific Revolution.

D.   Crusaders returned to Europe with more knowledge of Eastern Orthodox Christianity, contributing to the rites and teachings of the Catholic Church after centuries of stagnation following the fall of the Roman Empire.

30

Despite disorganization in the west, the Eastern Roman Empire was able to reorganize into the Byzantine Empire for which of the following reasons?

A.   Emperor Justinian's ability to establish rule of law

B.   a centralized seat of government in the Eastern Mediterranean, thanks to Constantine's having moved the imperial capital to Constantinople

C.   Justinian's consolidation of military power and ability to re-conquer parts of the Middle East and Northern Africa

D.   all of the above

WORLD HISTORY POST–1450 (30)

1

Which of the following best describes the motivation for Protestant reformers?

A. Protestants, including Martin Luther, originally sought to develop a new form of Christianity separate from the Catholic Church.

B. Protestants like Martin Luther were unhappy with the teachings of the church, including papal indulgences and corruption in the church, and originally sought reform.

C. Protestants were initially influenced by European political leaders, who used them to limit the power of the church.

D. Protestants, including Martin Luther, originally sought to topple the Catholic Church, believing it to have become too corrupt.

2

The Hundred Years' War

A. is an example of European unity against an outside, non-European invading force.

B. showed the technological dominance of the powers aligned with the Catholic Church, whose resources were massive.

C. indicated a shift in European politics from allegiance to one's ethnicity or nation to allegiance to the empire.

D. described ongoing ethnic conflict in Europe.

3

Major influences on the European Renaissance included

A. cultural discoveries in North America.

B. African music and culture.

C. Greek Orthodox Christianity and learning brought by Byzantine missionaries.

D. scientific knowledge from the Islamic empires and Greco-Roman philosophy and art.

4

Which of the following led to the French Revolution?

A. food shortages, heavy taxation of the peasants and bourgeoisie, and Enlightenment thought

B. the rise of Napoleon and militarization of French culture

C. the Congress of Vienna and shifting diplomatic alliances in Europe

D. the reign of Louis XIV

5

The Treaty of Westphalia

A. marked the end of the Thirty Years' War.

B. was indicative of a shift in European politics, towards international relations based on non-interference and emerging concepts of independent states, rather than empires dominated by the Catholic Church and other forces.

C. is often viewed as the foundation of modern European relations.

D. all of the above

6

Which of the following best describes the Counter-Reformation?

A. The Counter-Reformation was a response to corruption in the church that divided the Catholic Church.

B. The Counter-Reformation was a response to the Protestant Reformation.

C. The Counter-Reformation occurred in response to the discovery of the Americas.

D. The Counter-Reformation occurred in response to the Enlightenment.

7

How was Europe affected by the American Revolution?

A. Fearing a revolution at home, France supported the British.

B. Spain began decolonization in Latin America as a response to revolution in North America.

C. The ideals of the American Revolution inspired later revolutionary movements in Europe.

D. European powers ceased trade with the rebellious colonies.

8

How was Europe affected by the Civil War in the United States?

A. European powers were inspired to make slavery illegal following the American Civil War.

B. Industrializing European powers relied on Southern cotton, but were encouraged not to trade with the Confederacy so as not to support slavery, which had already been abolished in Europe and most European empires.

C. Industrializing European powers relied on Southern cotton, and traded with the Confederacy, supplying them with needed income during the Civil War.

D. None of the above are correct.

9

How did the United Kingdom reflect division in Europe and within Christianity in the seventeenth century?

A. Conflict between Protestants and Catholics over national leadership resulted in ongoing conflict and a series of unstable governments; however, following the Civil War, a Protestant monarchy was finally established in Great Britain and Ireland.

B. The purpose of the Glorious Revolution—to take back Protestant control of a Protestant country—was an example of the idea of the ethnic nation-state that was to take hold in Europe in later history.

C. Conflict between Protestants and Catholics over national leadership resulted in ongoing conflict and a series of unstable governments; however, following the Glorious Revolution, a Protestant monarchy was finally established.

D. While numerous Britons were Protestant, belonging to the church of England, Puritans feared an overwhelming Catholic influence and left for the North American colonies to create a new church.

10

Which of the following best describes the consequences of the Opium Wars?

A. British occupation of China

B. Chinese victory over Britain

C. unequal trade treaties favoring China

D. unequal trade treaties favoring Britain

11

European imperialism in the nineteenth century was a function of which of the following?

I. an effort to gain natural resources to power industrialization in the Americas

II. a way of shouldering the "white man's burden," or helping to improve "backward" societies

III. a competition between European countries to control territory, leading to phenomena like the "scramble for Africa"

A. I and II

B. II and III

C. I, II, and III

D. I and III

12

In the nineteenth century, Britain occupied parts of Somalia, Kenya, and Egypt, and negotiated boundaries and treaties with other colonial powers and local governments. Which of the following best explains why the British prioritized organizing this area?

A. Britain wished to safeguard shipping routes through the Red Sea and into the Indian Ocean.

B. Britain wished to control the valuable and popular routes in the Red Sea to Mecca and Medina.

C. Britain was concerned about instability in Somalia.

D. Britain was unable to consolidate control further inland into Africa.

13

During the 1884 Berlin Conference, European imperial powers

A. established extraterritoriality within important Chinese cities to support their nationals, who were participating in trade in opium, silk, and other Chinese goods.

B. agreed upon spheres of influence whereby each European country would dominate different parts of China.

C. determined which parts of Africa would be controlled by which European powers, a process also called the "scramble for Africa."

D. established the Triple Alliance and the Triple Entente, setting the stage for the system of alliances that would eventually spark the First World War.

14

As part of nineteenth-century European diplomacy in the tradition of the Congress of Vienna, how was the Three Emperors' League meant to maintain a balance of power?

A. Russia, Germany, and Austria-Hungary agreed that if one empire went to war, the other two would remain neutral; furthermore, the powers would consult with each other on matters of war.

B. Russia, Germany, and Austria-Hungary agreed that if one empire went to war, the other two would support it militarily; furthermore, the powers would consult with each other on matters of war.

C. Russia, Germany, and Austria-Hungary agreed that if one empire went to war, the other two would support it financially and with weaponry; furthermore, the powers would consult with each other on matters of war.

D. Russia, Germany, and Austria-Hungary agreed that an attack on one was an attack on all; furthermore, the three empires agreed not to levy taxes on one another to facilitate trade.

15

Choose the best description for the Russian strategy of empire-building.

A.   Russia focused on colonizing overseas, strengthening its navy to build a trans-oceanic empire.

B.   Russia focused on overland expansion, moving eastward into northern Asia across Siberia and westward into Eastern Europe.

C.   Russia remained isolated, avoiding expansion and focusing on industrialization instead.

D.   Russia lacked the resources to build an empire and struggled to maintain its agrarian-based society.

16

How were European empires affected by nationalism in the eighteenth and nineteenth centuries?

A.   European empires like the Austro-Hungarian Empire benefitted from nationalism, as Austrians and Hungarians were more loyal to the imperial government.

B.   The Austro-Hungarian Empire lost its Balkan territories to the Ottoman Empire, which was perceived to be more tolerant of Muslim minorities.

C.   Given the nature of empires—consolidated rule over an extended region home to diverse peoples—nationalism threatened empires as ethnic groups began to advocate for representation in imperial government.

D.   Given the nature of empires—consolidated rule over an extended region home to diverse peoples—nationalism threatened empires as ethnic groups began to advocate for their own independent states.

17

Following the collapse of the Ottoman Empire after the First World War, European countries took control of the Middle East, establishing protectorates according to arbitrary boundaries and installing rulers in accordance with European strategic interests. What effect has this had on the Middle East in the twentieth and twenty-first centuries?

A.   The Middle East has not been greatly affected.

B.   Illegitimate national borders and rulers have led to instability in the region.

C.   Improved governance, thanks to the protectorates, improved stability following the decline of the Ottoman Empire in the region.

D.   European investment in strategic resources supported long-term political stability in the Middle East.

18

The Meiji Restoration was

A.   a Japanese attempt to restore traditional Japan and reinvigorate Japanese culture as it had been before Western incursions into the country.

B.   a period of modernization and westernization in Japan.

C.   the early stage of Japanese imperialism in Asia, when it invaded Korea.

D.   a cultural movement in Japan to restore Shintoism and traditional poetry.

19

Choose the answer that presents events in the correct chronology:

A.   the French Revolution, the American Revolution, the Industrial Revolution, World War I

B.   the American Revolution, the French Revolution, Napoleon's conquests, World War I

C.   the French Revolution, the Industrial Revolution, the American Revolution, World War I

D.   the Rape of Nanjing, World War I, the Great Depression, World War II

20

Which of the following was not a consequence of nationalism in nineteenth-century Europe?

A.   Italian unification

B.   the Congress of Vienna

C.   German unification

D.   the Franco-Prussian War

21

Which of the following statements describes both the French Revolution and the Russian Revolution?

A.   Both originated among the wealthiest elites.

B.   Both valued agricultural workers over the middle class.

C.   Both sought a totally egalitarian society, with publicly owned means of production.

D.   Both were based upon ideals articulated by intellectuals who were not members of the working or agricultural classes.

22

Which of the following best explains the economic impact on Germany following the First World War?

A. Overspeculation on German farmland caused the market to crash.

B. Wartime reparations mandated by the Treaty of Versailles and the worldwide Great Depression caused inflation to skyrocket, plunging the German economy into crisis.

C. Germans were forced to pay extra taxes to cover reparations, and due to high prices, many could not afford to do so.

D. The Reichsmark was removed from circulation and replaced with the dollar as a means of punishment, forcing many Germans into poverty.

23

The Sino-Soviet Split was due in part to

A. the Chinese alliance with the United States.

B. the Soviet alliance with the United States.

C. the absence of the People's Republic of China from the United Nations.

D. division between the communist philosophies of Maoist China and the Marxist-Leninist USSR.

24

While the beginning of the Second World War is usually understood to be Hitler's invasion of Poland, some scholars date it even earlier. Which of the following events do some scholars identify as the beginning of World War II?

A. the Rape of Nanjing

B. the Japanese takeover of Korea

C. the Japanese invasion of Manchuria

D. the Chinese Civil War

25

Decolonization

A. was the process of granting independence to the European colonies in Africa, Asia, and the Pacific.

B. was overseen in great part by the United Nations.

C. was violent at times.

D. all of the above

26

Following the Soviet invasion of Afghanistan and subsequent withdrawal, Afghanistan

A.   came under Indian influence, making it vulnerable to extremist movements like the Taliban.

B.   descended into a period of instability and civil war, making it vulnerable to extremist movements like the Taliban.

C.   temporarily joined Pakistan in an effort to regain stability.

D.   temporarily came under NATO administration in an effort to regain stability and prevent the development of extremist groups.

27

Which of the following best describes the Warsaw Pact?

A.   a defense agreement between the Soviet Union and Eastern Bloc

B.   a Soviet alliance with Poland

C.   Soviet control over Eastern Europe

D.   the division of Eastern Europe after WWII

Read the excerpt and answer the questions that follow.

Somalia achieved its independence in 1960 with the union of Somalia, which had been under Italian administration as a United Nations trust territory, and Somaliland, which had been a British protectorate. The United States immediately established diplomatic relations with the new country. In 1969, the Somali army launched a coup which brought Mohamed Siad Barre to power. Barre adopted socialism and became allied with the Soviet Union. The United States was thus wary of Somalia in the period immediately after the coup.

Barre's government became increasingly radical in foreign affairs, and in 1977 launched a war against Ethiopia in hopes of claiming their territory. Ethiopia received help from the Soviet Union during the war, and so Somalia began to accept assistance from the United States, giving a new level of stability to the US-Somalia relationship.

Barre's dictatorship favored members of his own clan. In the 1980s, Somalis in less favored clans began to chafe under the government's rule. Barre's ruthlessness could not suppress the opposition, which in 1990 began to unify against him. After joining forces, the combined group of rebels drove Barre from Mogadishu in January 1991.

"Milestones 1993 – 2000: Somalia, 1992 – 1993,"
Office of the Historian, United States Department of State,
(last modified October 31, 2013).

28

In what way does Somalia show the impact of colonization on newly independent African countries?

A. Somalia had limited political infrastructure and civil society, making it vulnerable to a military coup by Mohamed Siad Barre.

B. Somalia had limited political infrastructure and civil society, and so it turned to the USSR for support in developing a sense of national unity and identity through socialism.

C. A sense of national Somali identity made it possible for Somaliland and the UN trust territory of Somalia to become a strong, unified nation-state.

D. Due to limited economic development (since most resources had gone to support the colonial powers), Somalia's infrastructure was weak; consequently, it strengthened its ties with the Cold War powers to support its economy by improving its position in international markets.

29

How is Somalia illustrative of a challenge faced by many former colonies in Africa?

A. Somalia's weak internal security has allowed piracy to flourish off of the coast of the Horn of Africa, posing a threat to shipping.

B. Somalia lacks a strong sense of national identity; people are more loyal to their own ethnic groups or clans than to a nation artificially created by colonial powers.

C. Newly independent Somalia, like many other African countries during decolonization, was forced to fight off the Cold War powers that were trying to gain influence in Africa.

D. Like many African countries, Somalia was unable to develop a strong presence at the United Nations.

30

Which of the following best describes the 1977 war between Somalia and Ethiopia in terms of the Cold War?

A. a proxy war in which the Soviet Union supported Ethiopia while the United States supported Somalia—only once did US and USSR military forces come into contact in Africa

B. an example of diplomacy where the USSR and US worked together to try to stop a war

C. a proxy war in which the Soviet Union supported Ethiopia while the United States supported Somalia—US and USSR military forces were not directly involved in the fighting

D. The 1977 war was not relevant to the Cold War.

US History to 1877 (30)

1

Why was the Mayflower Compact an important contribution to the foundation of American government?

A.   It provided for equal treatment of all Christians under the law.

B.   It was the first treaty between European settlers (the Pilgrims) and Native Americans.

C.   It laid out terms for government with the consent of the governed.

D.   It allowed people of all faiths to practice their religions freely under the law.

2

How did the colonies in New England differ from southern ones like Virginia, the Carolinas, and Georgia?

A.   Farms tended to be larger in the southern colonies and produce cash crops like tobacco using slave labor; in the north, smaller family farms predominated, and early urbanization was more widespread.

B.   Farms tended to be larger in the northern colonies and produce cash crops like tobacco, using slave labor; in the south, smaller family farms predominated, and early urbanization was more widespread.

C.   The southern colonies were wealthier than the northern colonies, with a more educated population.

D.   There were no major differences between the northern and southern colonies before independence.

3

What advantage did the colonists have in the American Revolution?

A.   vast financial wealth

B.   superior weaponry

C.   strong leadership and knowledge of the terrain

D.   a professional military and access to mercenaries

4

What resources attracted the French and the British to North America?

A.   tobacco

B.   rice

C.   beaver pelts

D.   all of the above

5

The British and French leveraged alliances with which of the following tribes in conflicts in colonial North America?

A. the Sioux and the Cheyenne

B. the Algonquin and the Iroquois

C. the Cherokee and the Seminole

D. the Apache and the Miami

6

How did the views of the Federalists and the Anti-Federalists differ during the Constitutional Convention?

A. The views of the Federalists and Anti-Federalists did not significantly differ at the Constitutional Convention.

B. The Anti-Federalists did not believe in a Constitution at all, while the Federalists insisted on including the Bill of Rights.

C. The Anti-Federalists favored a stronger Constitution and federal government, while Federalists were concerned that states would risk losing their autonomy.

D. The Federalists favored a stronger Constitution and federal government, while Anti-Federalists were concerned that states would risk losing their autonomy.

7

The early Democratic Party (the Democratic-Republicans) was mainly concerned with which of the following?

A. agrarian issues, small landowners, and maintaining a weaker federal government

B. fiscal policy in support of urban areas and big businesses

C. limitations on federal oversight of business and banks

D. maintaining a strong federal government

8

What was one reason for the election of Andrew Jackson?

A. Jackson was able to find a solution to the first Nullification Crisis.

B. Allowing those white males who did not own property to vote was a boon to Jackson, who was popular with the "common man."

C. Jackson's popularity with landowners in Northern states guaranteed him the funds he needed to win the presidency.

D. Jackson and his vice president, John C. Calhoun, were a strong and popular team when running for election.

9

Which of the following best describes the conditions faced by Latinos and Latinas who had remained in western territories won by the US in the Mexican-American War?

A.   They were treated with derision; many lost land and wealth they had held under Mexico, and did not enjoy the same rights under the law as citizens, even though they had been promised American citizenship in the Treaty of Guadalupe Hidalgo.

B.   While many had lost land and wealth they had held under Mexico, they were entitled to and received restitution from the government of the United States.

C.   They were treated equally in social and political situations under the United States.

D.   Most Latinos and Latinas left the western territories for Mexico following the Mexican-American War, due to discriminatory conditions they faced under the United States government.

10

Which of the following is a safeguard against federal overreach built into the US Constitution?

A.   a system of checks and balances, in which a president can only be elected to two consecutive terms

B.   a system of checks and balances, in which the House, Senate, and president are able to limit each other

C.   a system of checks and balances, in which the president—a civilian leader—controls the military

D.   a system of checks and balances, in which the three branches of government—executive, legislative, and judicial—are able to limit each other

11

John Adams would have been likely to agree with which of the following statements?

A.   A strong federal government is necessary to keep the United States together as one country.

B.   States' rights are paramount.

C.   The Bill of Rights was always intended to be part of the US Constitution.

D.   The Articles of Confederation sufficed to assert the sovereignty of the United States of America.

12

In the first half of the nineteenth century, social change in the US was driven by religious and social organizations that helped to foster political interest in women's rights, abolitionism, and utopianism. This movement was called:

A.   the Industrial Revolution

B.   the Second Great Awakening

C.   the Enlightenment

D.   the Glorious Revolution

13

With the Monroe Doctrine, President Monroe attempted to

A.   keep the United States involved in European conflicts.

B.   isolate the United States from European intervention in its affairs.

C.   assert US hegemony in the Western Hemisphere by isolating it from Europe, to prevent European powers from expanding there.

D.   increase US involvement in international affairs.

14

The Louisiana Purchase was controversial most especially because of

A.   the difficult relationship between the United States and France.

B.   concerns about federal overreach, given the scope of the purchase.

C.   concerns about maintaining stable relationships with the Native Americans living in the territories west of the Mississippi River.

D.   the amount of land it encompassed and the ability of the US to bring it under control.

15

Which of the following best explains the Three-Fifths Compromise?

A.   Three-fifths of the states would be permitted to own slaves.

B.   Three-fifths of the states needed to ratify amendments before they could go into effect.

C.   To account for a state's population size, a slave would count for three-fifths of a person.

D.   Three-fifths of the states had to ratify the Constitution before it could go into effect.

16

An important benefit of the Louisiana Purchase was

A.   possession of Texas.

B.   access to the Pacific Ocean.

C.   total control over the Oregon Trail.

D.   control over the Port of New Orleans and the Mississippi River.

17

Which group insisted on including the Bill of Rights in the Constitution in order to ratify it?

A.   Constitutionalists

B.   Revolutionaries

C.   Federalists

D.   Anti-Federalists

18

The strategic alliance between the British and Tecumseh's Confederacy

A.   helped the British win the War of 1812.

B.   was part of Tecumseh's plan, along with the allied tribes, to form a sovereign nation northwest of the United States.

C.   was intended to mislead the British, when in reality Tecumseh had secretly formed an alliance with the US

D.   caused the breakdown of the British army.

19

How did the Fugitive Slave Act empower slave states under federal law?

A.   Slave states had the right to take escaped slaves to court under the Fugitive Slave Act; even though the former slaves were safe in free states, they were still subject to prosecution and in danger of being legally returned to their former "masters" if they were unable to prove residency in a free state.

B.   Despite the reluctance of states' rights advocates—many of whom were based in slave states—to adhere to federal law, many of these same advocates approved of the federal Fugitive Slave Act because it allowed them to pursue escaped slaves from slave states to free states and to capture them.

C.   Slave states were able to send police and military authorities into free states to capture escaped slaves.

D.   Slave states were able to prosecute free states in federal court for offering safe haven to escaped slaves.

20

What assets did the Confederacy have during the Civil War?

A.   The Confederacy had superior weaponry and production resources.

B.   The Confederacy maintained brisk trade with Europe, enabling it to fund the war.

C.   The Confederacy benefitted from strong military leadership and high morale among the population.

D.   The Confederacy's strong infrastructure allowed it to transport supplies and people efficiently throughout the South.

21

How did the Dred Scott decision affect the Fugitive Slave Act?

A.   It weakened the act.

B.   It strengthened the act.

C.   It had no effect on the act.

D.   It abolished the act.

22

The Compromises of 1820 and 1850, and the Kansas-Nebraska Act all revolved around which of the following issues?

A.   states' rights to legalize slavery

B.   accommodating politicians who protected slavery and the rights of their states to keep its practice legal

C.   deep division within the United States over the role of the federal government, as illustrated by the question of states' rights to legalize slavery

D.   all of the above

23

Why was the principle of popular sovereignty controversial?

A.   Slave owners were concerned that free black Americans would vote against slavery in new states.

B.   White settlers were concerned that they would be outnumbered by Native Americans in new states and therefore have less political control.

C.   Mormon settlers in the Utah Territory were concerned that non-Mormon settlers moving westward due to the act would have too much influence in local politics.

D.   Popular sovereignty allowed the legality of slavery in new states to be decided by those able to vote, when it was originally to have been outlawed in new states.

24

Which of the following effectively repealed the Missouri Compromise?

A. the Dred Scott decision

B. the Compromise of 1850

C. the Kansas-Nebraska Act

D. the Fugitive Slave Act

25

Which of the following best explains the strategy behind the Anaconda Plan?

A. The North would "squeeze" the South by taking control of the Mississippi River and establishing a naval blockade on the Atlantic coast; given the South's reliance on cotton export for revenue, this would be a devastating economic blow.

B. The North would "squeeze" the South by taking control of the Mississippi River and establishing a naval blockade on the Atlantic coast; given the South's reliance on raw materials from overseas to power its industrial growth, this would be a devastating economic blow.

C. The North would crush Southern resistance by fighting primarily in Virginia; by "squeezing" the seat of Confederate government in Richmond, it hoped to cause the entire Confederacy to collapse.

D. The North would surround the South with troops in Kentucky, West Virginia, Missouri, and elsewhere, hoping to outnumber their forces.

26

A major consequence of the Civil War was

A. the rise of the Federalist Party.

B. the destruction of the South's economy and the growth of the North's economy.

C. the emergence of the Republican Party.

D. the growth of the South's economy and the destruction of the North's economy.

27

The Reconstruction Acts

A. immediately improved conditions for African Americans in the South.

B. immediately benefitted the Southern economy.

C. were widely considered fair in Congress and by Southerners.

D. imposed Northern military control over the South.

28

Following the Civil War, the United States ratified the Thirteenth, Fourteenth and Fifteenth Amendments to the Constitution. What did these amendments guarantee?

A.   an end to slavery, equal rights for all Americans, and voting rights for all Americans, respectively

B.   an end to slavery, equal rights for all Americans, and voting rights for all African Americans, respectively

C.   an end to slavery, equal rights for all American men, and voting rights for all African American men, respectively

D.   an end to slavery, equal rights for Americans, and voting rights for African American men, respectively

29

Even after the end of slavery, African Americans in the rural South still suffered due to

A.   sharecropping, which kept them in heavy debt, often to their former "masters."

B.   the Colored Farmers' Alliance, which was organized to limit their efforts to become independent farmers.

C.   the Reconstruction Acts, which specifically punished Southern blacks who did not join the Union army.

D.   labor unions, which advocated for white workers' rights in factories in urban areas and ignored rural issues.

30

How did the Bureau of Indian Affairs break down tribal bonds and weaken Native American societies?

A.   through policies of assimilation

B.   by forcing Native American children to go to white schools and reject their cultures

C.   by forcing Native Americans to move onto reservations

D.   all of the above

US HISTORY 1877–PRESENT (30)

1

The United States remained relatively neutral in international conflicts for much of its early history; its first major assertion of international power and foreign intervention overseas is considered to be which of the following?

A.   the Spanish-American War

B.   the First World War

C.   the Texan Revolution

D.   the War of 1812

2

Within the two years following the WWI, the US would

A.   join the League of Nations.

B.   join NATO.

C.   ratify the Treaty of Versailles.

D.   none of the above

3

Antitrust legislation in the US was designed to

A.   reduce wealth.

B.   redistribute wealth.

C.   prevent businesses from monopolizing and thus disrupt the market.

D.   prevent price controls.

4

Which of the following best explains why the Temperance movement became popular?

A.   Because women were discouraged from public consumption of alcohol, women activists in the Progressive movement felt that prohibition of consumption of alcoholic beverages would encourage social equality.

B.   High prices for alcohol were an increasing problem for working class families, for whom this product was one of few affordable luxuries.

C.   Alcohol consumption by working men, generally the breadwinners in impoverished urban households, affected their wives and female partners, who were forced to cope with the resulting strain on household budgets and domestic violence.

D.   Since most alcohol was imported from overseas, a movement to decrease trade with European powers was popular with nationalists.

5

Women did not receive full suffrage in the United States until which of the following?

A.   The Seneca Falls Convention was held.

B.   The Nineteenth Amendment was ratified.

C.   The Equal Rights Amendment was ratified.

D.   The Voting Rights Act of 1965 was passed.

6

Nineteenth-century workers organized labor unions for all of the following reasons except for which of the following?

A.   they were not paid fairly for their work

B.   their shifts were frequently 12 – 14 hours a day

C.   to overthrow capitalists like Carnegie and Rockefeller

D.   dangerous work conditions

7

Which of the following best describes Social Darwinism?

A.   the belief in evolution

B.   the belief that survival of the fittest applies to communities of people, particularly as regards race or wealth

C.   a rejection of the theory of evolution

D.   the belief that evolution applies only to creatures and not social groups

8

The Cuban Missile Crisis ultimately resulted in

A.   the installation of the Castro regime.

B.   the fall of the Castro regime.

C.   a new opening of dialogue between the United States and the Soviet Union.

D.   the end of a period of détente between the United States and the Soviet Union.

9

SALT and SALT II were indicative of what in the US – USSR relationship?

A.   a stalemate

B.   a period of conflict

C.   glasnost

D.   a period of diplomatic détente

10

President Theodore Roosevelt, a Progressive, was known for which major action?

A.   prosecuting the Northern Securities Company under the Interstate Commerce Act, breaking up this large monopoly and earning his reputation as a "trust-buster"

B.   developing the Works Progress Administration to assist working people in finding jobs and to support mistreated factory workers

C.   ensuring the ratification of the Sixteenth Amendment

D.   limiting the use of the Sherman Antitrust Act only to a few situations, earning his reputation as a "trust-buster"

11

During periods of high tension between the United States and the Soviet Union in the 1950s, how was the US affected?

A.   Fear of communism was pervasive, and during the McCarthy era, accusations were made against public figures.

B.   Fearing Soviet communism, the United States supported Maoism in China as a counterweight to Leninism.

C.   During the McCarthy hearings, several members of Congress were found to be communist and so were removed from office.

D.   During the McCarthy hearings, several members of Congress were found to be Soviet spies and so were removed from office.

12

The Iranian hostage crisis

A.   resulted in the establishment of an anti-American theocracy in Iran.

B.   contributed to the election of Ronald Reagan to the presidency, which led to the escalation of weapons production and the arms race.

C.   resulted in regional instability, forcing the Soviet invasion of Afghanistan.

D.   contributed to the election of Jimmy Carter to the presidency, which led to a period of détente with the Soviet Union.

13

How did internment affect Japanese-Americans?

A.   The US government immediately compensated them after the war.

B.   They did not fight internment in court.

C.   Many lost their property and were treated as potential traitors.

D.   They were forcibly relocated to the East Coast.

14

A consequence of US support for Israel in the Six-Day and Yom Kippur Wars was

A.   OPEC's oil embargo, which was economically harmful for the Middle East.

B.   OPEC's oil embargo, which was economically harmful for many working Americans.

C.   increased Arab support for the United States in international forums like the United Nations.

D.   improved relations between the United States, Saudi Arabia, and Iran.

15

Which of the following were part of the War on Poverty?

I.   Head Start

II.   Department of Housing and Urban Development

III. Social Security

A.   I and II

B.   I and III

C.   II and III

D.   I, II, and III

16

Cesar Chavez and the United Farm Workers

A.   supported Mexicans who wanted to join the Bracero Program and become guest workers in the United States.

B.   supported Mexican-American agricultural workers in California and the Southwest, and also provided a foundation for later advocacy groups supporting the rights of Hispanic Americans.

C.   worked on behalf of Texas farmers to coordinate agreements with agricultural workers from Mexico.

D.   none of the above

17

Which of the following is generally considered to mark the beginning of the movement for LGBT civil rights in the US?

A.   the first Gay Pride marches in New York, Chicago, and San Francisco

B.   the election of Harvey Milk to the San Francisco Board of Supervisors

C.   activism and dialogue surrounding the AIDS crisis

D.   the Stonewall Riots

18

Which of the following best explains the difference between the philosophies of the Rev. Dr. Martin Luther King Jr. and Malcolm X?

A.   Dr. King believed that African Americans should focus on empowering black communities, while Malcolm X believed that African Americans should focus on racial integration.

B.   Dr. King believed that African Americans should focus on racial integration, while Malcolm X believed that African Americans should focus on empowering black communities.

C.   Dr. King believed that African Americans should focus on political change, while Malcolm X believed that African Americans should focus on social change.

D.   Dr. King and Malcolm X did not differ in their philosophies on civil rights.

19

Which of the following best explains the impact of the Watergate scandal on the United States?

A.   President Nixon was impeached.

B.   President Nixon declined to seek a second term of office.

C.   Americans lost faith in the federal government.

D.   Americans began supporting third-party candidates more.

20

Which of the following is a hallmark of conservative ideology?

A.   open borders to facilitate international trade

B.   low taxes

C.   labor rights

D.   a small, efficient military

21

The United States invaded Afghanistan following the terrorist attacks of September 11, 2001

A.   in order to defeat the Taliban, who had attacked the United States.

B.   in order to capture Osama bin Laden and al Qaeda, who had attacked the United States and who were harbored by the Taliban, the government of Afghanistan.

C.   in order to defeat al Qaeda, the government of Afghanistan.

D.   in order to defeat al Qaeda, which held weapons of mass destruction in Afghanistan.

22

The Patriot Act was controversial because it

A. permitted the US to search for weapons of mass destruction in Iraq, following the terrorist attacks on September 11, 2001; however, many believed that Iraq had not been involved in planning these attacks.

B. expanded the NSA's ability to spy on foreign heads of state, a violation of international law.

C. established Guantanamo Bay as a detention center for suspected terrorists captured in the War on Terror but without allowing them visits from the International Committee of the Red Cross, a violation of the Geneva Convention.

D. broadened the government's powers of surveillance over the activities of American citizens, interpreted as a violation of Americans' rights under the Fourth Amendment and other rights to privacy.

23

Why was the prison opened at the US naval base at Guantanamo Bay, Cuba, following the terrorist attacks of September 11, 2001, so controversial?

A. Surveillance programs secretly run from the prison at Guantanamo were found to have violated privacy laws in the United States.

B. Both Democrats and Republicans argued that prisoners at Guantanamo Bay should be moved to prisons within the United States to save money, as the facility at Guantanamo was enormously expensive.

C. Prisoners at Guantanamo Bay were denied the rights normally granted to prisoners of war under the Geneva Convention, to which the United States is a party.

D. Many US citizens were found to have been mistakenly imprisoned in Guantanamo for crimes they did not commit.

24

The United States invaded and occupied Iraq during Operation Iraqi Freedom in 2003

A. under the faulty premise that Saddam Hussein held weapons of mass destruction and was linked to al Qaeda, which had recently attacked the US.

B. in order to capture Osama bin Laden, who was under the protection of Saddam Hussein.

C. after it was proven that Iraq provided al Qaeda with weapons it used to attack the United States on 9/11.

D. because Iraq attacked the United States on September 11, 2001.

25

Which of the following best describes the approach taken by the Reagan administration to counter the Soviet Union?

A.   bilateral diplomacy

B.   direct military confrontation

C.   engagement in multilateral fora such as the United Nations

D.   escalation of arms production and proxy warfare

Read the excerpt and answer the questions that follow.

To ensure the peaceful development of nations, free from coercion, the United States has taken a leading part in establishing the United Nations. The United Nations is designed to make possible lasting freedom and independence for all its members. We shall not realize our objectives, however, unless we are willing to help free peoples to maintain their free institutions and their national integrity against aggressive movements that seek to impose upon them totalitarian regimes. This is no more than a frank recognition that totalitarian regimes imposed on free peoples, by direct or indirect aggression, undermine the foundations of international peace and hence the security of the United States.

The peoples of a number of countries of the world have recently had totalitarian regimes forced upon them against their will. The Government of the United States has made frequent protests against coercion and intimidation, in violation of the Yalta agreement, in Poland, Rumania, and Bulgaria. I must also state that in a number of other countries there have been similar developments.

At the present moment in world history nearly every nation must choose between alternative ways of life. The choice is too often not a free one.

One way of life is based upon the will of the majority, and is distinguished by free institutions, representative government, free elections, guarantees of individual liberty, freedom of speech and religion, and freedom from political oppression.

The second way of life is based upon the will of a minority forcibly imposed upon the majority. It relies upon terror and oppression, a controlled press and radio; fixed elections, and the suppression of personal freedoms.

I believe that it must be the policy of the United States to support free peoples who are resisting attempted subjugation by armed minorities or by outside pressures.

80th Cong. 171 (1947) (Statement of Harry Truman, President of the United States)
March 12, 1947 (Truman Doctrine)

26

How does Truman differentiate between the two ways of life he discusses in his speech?

A.   He describes one as better than the other.

B.   He describes one as based on free institutions, speech, elections, religion, but politically oppressive, while the other is based on oppression, suppressed radio, press, and personal freedoms, but with some political freedoms.

C.   He describes one free from political oppression, and the other with only limited political freedoms.

D.   He describes one as based on free institutions, speech, elections, religion, and freedom from political oppression, while the other is based on oppression, rigged elections, and suppressed radio, press, and personal freedoms.

27

Read this sentence from the text.

This is no more than a frank recognition that totalitarian regimes imposed on free peoples, by direct or indirect aggression, undermine the foundations of international peace and hence the security of the United States.

In the context of the excerpt, how is this idea comparable to the Bush doctrine of preemption?

A.   It argues that communism is a threat to US security.

B.   It states that the US must protect its national sovereignty.

C.   It argues that the US must intervene in countries before they are taken over by totalitarian forces; otherwise, national security is at risk.

D.   It argues that the US must intervene in countries after they are taken over by totalitarian forces; otherwise, national security is at risk.

28

When discussing the "two ways of life," what is Truman describing?

A.   the differences between communism and democratic capitalism—that is, between the US and the USSR

B.   the differences between communism and democratic totalitarianism—that is, between the USSR and the European Union

C.   the differences between communism and fascism—that is, between the USSR and Nazi Germany

D.   the differences between democratic capitalism and fascism—that is, between the US and the USSR

29

Read this excerpt from the text.

> The peoples of a number of countries of the world have recently had totalitarian regimes forced upon them against their will. The Government of the United States has made frequent protests against coercion and intimidation, in violation of the Yalta agreement, in Poland, Rumania, and Bulgaria. I must also state that in a number of other countries there have been similar developments.

To which historical developments is Truman referring?

A.   the occupation of the Sudetenland and Poland, among other European countries, by Hitler

B.   the occupation of several Eastern European countries by Stalin

C.   the construction of the Berlin Wall and the occupation of Poland, Romania, and Bulgaria by the USSR

D.   the construction of the Iron Curtain

30

A historian of the Cold War would most likely use this excerpt from Truman's speech in order to help answer which of the following questions?

A.   How did the United States determine its foreign policy following the Second World War?

B.   What were the two ways of life available to the world following the Second World War?

C.   What is the purpose of the United Nations?

D.   What were twentieth-century American values?

Answer Key

WORLD HISTORY PRE-1450

1)

    A.   Incorrect. The Hittites expanded overland.

    B.   **Correct.** The Hittites were skilled charioteers and were early pioneers of iron weaponry.

    C.   Incorrect. The Hittites created their own weapons; furthermore, they preceded ancient Greek development.

    D.   Incorrect. The Hittites worked with iron.

2)

    A.   Incorrect. The Peloponnesian War was between Sparta and Athens, not Sparta and Crete.

    B.   Incorrect. The Peloponnesian War was fought between Greeks in Peloponnesus and Central Greece, not in Anatolia.

    C.   Incorrect. The Peloponnesian War did not involve Persia.

    D.   **Correct.** The Peloponnesian War was between the major Greek powers.

3)

    A.   **Correct.** Developing agricultural practices in the Neolithic Era allowed humans to establish settled societies sustained by reliable food sources.

    B.   Incorrect. While the wheel was an important development in the Neolithic Era, it was just one part of the major change in human behavior exhibited in that era: the development of settled societies.

C.   Incorrect. The use of bronze was a defining characteristic of the eponymous Bronze Age, which followed the Neolithic Era.

D.   Incorrect. While it is likely that early medical treatment developed in the Neolithic Era, again, this was not a defining characteristic of this period; furthermore it was made possible by the development of settled societies.

4)

A.   Incorrect. In the Neolithic Era, only *Homo sapiens* would exist, but during the Paleolithic Era, other hominids existed.

B.   Correct. During the Paleolithic Era, hominids like *Australopithecus* and later, *Homo habilis*, *Homo erectus*, *Homo neanderthalensis* lived.

C.   Incorrect. Humans began changing their behavior; eventually *Homo sapiens* would begin to practice agriculture and settle communities while other hominids would die out. It is still not clear why other hominids died out or, indeed, whether they coexisted with our ancestors at all (although it seems possible that *Homo sapiens* and *Homo neanderthalensis* did coexist).

D.   Incorrect. A number of early humans coexisted and were evolving.

5)

A.   Correct. By the Neolithic Era, other hominids had died out.

B.   Incorrect. Other hominids did not survive beyond the Paleolithic Era.

C.   Incorrect. It is unclear why other hominids died out.

D.   Incorrect. *Homo sapiens* existed.

6)

A.   Incorrect. Development of bronze metallurgy was widespread.

B.   Incorrect. Evidence of bronze metallurgy has been found throughout Eurasia.

C.   Correct. Humans began using bronze globally and concurrently.

D.   Incorrect. Several different civilizations used bronze.

7)

A.   Correct. The caste system is a social hierarchy rooted in religious tradition. It is not possible to change the caste into which one is born.

B.   Incorrect. While the caste system is a social hierarchy, and while there is more social and economic flexibility within it than before, it is not possible to move from one caste to another.

C.   Incorrect. One's position in the hierarchy is determined by birth; a person is born into his or her caste, and that position is permanent.

D.   Incorrect. While this definition is true, it leaves out the traditionally religious nature of the caste system.

8)

A.   Incorrect. While early Chinese and Fertile Crescent civilizations were both organized under an emperor or king, this answer choice is incomplete.

B.   Incorrect. Again, while these civilizations did both have written languages, this answer choice is also incomplete, given the other possible responses.

C.   Incorrect. Monotheism did not exist in either of these regions, aside from Judaism practiced by the Hebrews, a small tribe in the Levant who were not politically powerful.

D.   Correct. China and the Fertile Crescent civilizations like the Sumerians, Assyrians, Babylonians, Egyptians, and Akkadians had imperial or monarchical governments; they also developed written languages.

9)

A.   Incorrect. Early societies in the Fertile Crescent developed irrigation before developing bronze.

B.   Incorrect. The Neolithic Era preceded the Bronze Age.

C.   Incorrect. Copper is a naturally occurring element, from which humans create bronze.

D.   Correct. Bronze improved weapons and tools; improved weaponry meant expanded control over territory and more secure societies that could continue to develop.

10)

A.   Incorrect. Confucianism emerged in China during the Spring and Autumn Period, before the Qin dynasty.

B.   Incorrect. Written Chinese is believed to have developed as early as the Shang dynasty period, several centuries earlier.

C.   Correct. Under the Qin dynasty, the emperor centralized Chinese bureaucracy and standardized weights and measures in order to centralize and consolidate imperial power.

D.   Incorrect. A and B are incorrect.

11)

A.   Correct. Early Chinese writing evolved under the Shang dynasty.

B.   Incorrect. The Mandate of Heaven developed under the Zhou dynasty.

C.   Incorrect. The Forbidden City was constructed under the Ming dynasty.

D.   Incorrect. Only choice A is correct.

12)

    A.   Incorrect. Several early civilizations in the Fertile Crescent developed irrigation.

    B.   Incorrect. The Sumerians developed cuneiform.

    C.   **Correct.** King Hammurabi's code meted out justice on an equal basis ("an eye for an eye, a tooth for a tooth").

    D.   Incorrect. The Hittites mastered iron weaponry and charioteering.

13)

    A.   Incorrect. This answer describes East Asia.

    B.   **Correct.** This describes the traditional Caste system of the subcontinent.

    C.   Incorrect. While Buddhism emerged in India, it is more widely practiced in East and Southeast Asia.

    D.   Incorrect. China had an exam-based administrative hierarchy.

14)

    A.   **Correct.** Buddhism, though it emerged in India, is mainly practiced throughout the Himalayas, East Asia, and Southeast Asia.

    B.   Incorrect. While Buddhism developed in India, it is not widely practiced there.

    C.   Incorrect. Buddhism is practiced throughout Tibet, East Asia, and Southeast Asia.

    D.   Incorrect. Buddhism is widespread not only in Southeast Asia, but also in East Asia and Tibet.

15)

    A.   Incorrect. The Magyars did not topple the Holy Roman Empire; furthermore, their incursions into Europe had been several hundred years prior.

    B.   **Correct.** The continental—indeed, global—impact of the Black Death destabilized much of Europe.

    C.   Incorrect. The Black Death actually destabilized the Mongol Empire.

    D.   Incorrect. The Umayyads reached Iberia long before the Black Death.

16)

    A.   Incorrect. The Catholic Church gained power and became an important stabilizing force in Western Europe.

    B.   Incorrect. The Byzantine Empire expanded in the Balkans, the Middle East, and North Africa.

C.   Incorrect. The Holy Roman Empire was consolidated later under Otto I in 962.

D.   Correct. Charlemagne was Frankish and stabilized parts of Western and Central Europe; most of the Carolingian Empire eventually became France.

17)

A.   Incorrect. Venice was not a major global colonial power, nor did it develop mercantilism.

B.   Incorrect. While Venice was a center of intellectual and cultural development, this was not a major reason for development of modern banking there.

C.   Correct. As a commercial center and well-situated to handle goods arriving in Europe from the Silk Road and from Africa, Venice developed banking institutions that influenced modern banking.

D.   Incorrect. As a center of international trade, Venice was strongly affected by the plague.

18)

A.   Incorrect. While the time the Jewish people spent in Egypt is an important part of Jewish history, Judaism developed in Southwest Asia, not North Africa.

B.   Correct. Judaism emerged in the area that is today home to Israelis and Palestinians.

C.   Incorrect. The Jewish presence in Mesopotamia was a key time in Jewish history; however, Judaism did not emerge there.

D.   Incorrect. The Levant can be considered part of the Fertile Crescent; however, B is the better answer because it is more specific. In the case of a question where more than one answer could be chosen, however, both of these answers would be correct.

19)

A.   Incorrect. Serfs, while limited in their freedom, were not truly slaves; they could not be bought or sold.

B.   Correct. Serfs were bonded to the land—they had to work it for the lord—however, the lord was obligated to protect them.

C.   Incorrect. Serfs did not fight.

D.   Incorrect. Serfs could not purchase individual freedom by fighting for their lords.

20)

    A.   Incorrect. Both Sunnis and Shi'ites believed in extending Islam everywhere beyond the Arabian Peninsula.

    B.   Incorrect. Both Sunnis and Shi'ites agreed that military conquest was vital in order to spread Islam.

    C.   Incorrect. Both Sunnis and Shi'ites agreed with the teachings of Muhammad, including the philosophy of the "People of the Book."

    D.   **Correct.** Sunnis believed that the Meccan elites should take over leadership of Muslims, while Shi'ite believed that Muhammad's cousin Ali was Muhammad's rightful successor.

21)

    A.   Incorrect. Crusaders returned to Europe having been exposed to learning and technology in the Middle East that was, at the time, unknown in Europe.

    B.   **Correct.** European powers controlled some areas in the Levant, but only temporarily.

    C.   Incorrect. Crusaders were entitled to indulgences—forgiveness for any sins committed in conflict.

    D.   Incorrect. One incentive for Europeans to fight in the Crusades was the possibility of amassing personal wealth through plunder.

22)

    A.   Incorrect. Russia eventually embraced Orthodox Christianity, which was originally introduced to Russia as Greek Orthodox Christianity as practiced by the Byzantines.

    B.   Incorrect. Vladimir I did not convert to Catholicism.

    C.   **Correct.** Byzantine missionaries spread Orthodox Christianity north; Vladimir I converted and a tradition of Orthodox Christianity took root in Russia and Ukraine.

    D.   Incorrect. Russia's Orthodox tradition came from Byzantium.

23)

    A.   Incorrect. Mongol power had actually been a factor in the decline of the Abbasids.

    B.   Incorrect. The Yuan dynasty was a Mongol dynasty.

    C.   **Correct.** Ivan the Great had weakened Mongol power in Northwest Asia, while the Ming had taken control of China from the Mongols.

    D.   Incorrect. The Abbasid Caliphate was a non-factor in Mongol decline, while Ivan the Great played an important role in it.

24)

    A.   **Correct.** Papal endorsement of Charlemagne gave his rule legitimacy.

    B.   Incorrect. Charlemagne did not promise to end the feudal system, which actually brought stability to Europe.

    C.   Incorrect. The Crusades did not begin until 1096. Charlemagne was crowned in 800.

    D.   Incorrect. Charlemagne was supported by the church.

25)

    A.   Incorrect. Both churches were powerful in their respective regions.

    B.   **Correct.** At the time, the pope controlled the Papal States in Italy, which were political territories; furthermore, he was extremely influential among European leaders.

    C.   Incorrect. While Rome was a significant city, this was not the reason for the church's power; the importance of Christianity among Europeans was.

    D.   Incorrect. The pope was extremely influential; however his political control was generally indirect.

26)

    A.   Incorrect. While fighters were promised indulgences, this was not the only encouragement they received to fight in the Crusades.

    B.   Incorrect. Amassing wealth was an incentive to join the Crusades, but it was not the only one.

    C.   Incorrect. Many fighters were driven by their faith to counter perceived threats to Christianity, but this answer choice is incomplete given the other options available.

    D.   **Correct.** All of the answer choices are true.

27)

    A.   Incorrect. The Ming dynasty consolidated power in China; Ivan the Great controlled Russia as the Mongols went into decline.

    B.   Incorrect. The Qin constructed the Great Wall.

    C.   **Correct.** Ming power extended into Southeast Asia, Central Asia, and Korea; the Ming developed trade and exacted tribute from local leaders.

    D.   Incorrect. While the Ming encouraged oceanic exploration, they did not develop a major navy.

28)

    A.   Incorrect. Mali did not control the trans-Saharan trade routes.

    B.   Incorrect. The Kingdom of Mali embraced Islam.

C.   **Correct.** Mali became wealthy due to gold and salt, valuable natural resources.

D.   Incorrect. Mali did not control the trans-Saharan trade routes.

29)

A.   Incorrect. Fighters did not return with Middle Eastern wives and diversity in Europe did not increase.

B.   Incorrect. While some returning Europeans had learned a new language, this alone was not enough of a widespread phenomenon to impact international trade.

C.   **Correct.** Crusaders had gained knowledge of navigation, technology, medicine, and science—incidentally, all knowledge and skills necessary in warfare—and transferred this knowledge to Europe, helping spark the Scientific Revolution and the Renaissance.

D.   Incorrect. In fact, at times the Orthodox Church and the Catholic Church worked together against Muslims.

30)

A.   Incorrect. Justinian's strong leadership and rule of law undoubtedly contributed to the stability of the Byzantine Empire, but the empire enjoyed other advantages, too.

B.   Incorrect. Constantinople was situated very strategically; however, the city's location was not the only reason for Byzantine success.

C.   Incorrect. Justinian was able to expand Byzantine territory, but the empire would not have been sustainable without other advantages.

D.   **Correct.** All of the answer choices present essential factors in Byzantine organization and stability in the face of decline in the West.

WORLD HISTORY POST–1450

1)
    A.   Incorrect. Martin Luther was a Catholic monk; he originally sought reform within the Catholic Church.

    B.   **Correct.** Martin Luther and his followers opposed corruption in the church and wanted changes.

    C.   Incorrect. The Reformation was not originally a political movement.

    D.   Incorrect. Again, Martin Luther wanted reform, not to overthrow the papacy or the church.

2)
    A.   Incorrect. The Hundred Years' War was an intra-European war.

    B.   Incorrect. The Hundred Years' War occurred before the Reformation and was a conflict mainly between England and France; the church was not a major figure.

    C.   Incorrect. This was not a factor of the Hundred Years' War.

    D.   **Correct.** The Hundred Years' War was really an ongoing conflict between different European ethnic groups (mainly, the French and the English).

3)
    A.   Incorrect. While the Americas were of interest to many Renaissance figures, the historical movement did not rely on developments in the Western Hemisphere.

    B.   Incorrect. African music and culture had no bearing on the Renaissance.

    C.   Incorrect. While Christians came from Constantinople following its conquest by the Ottomans, their influence on the Renaissance came from the classical texts and learning they brought, not from their Christian faith.

    D.   **Correct.** Science and technology imported from the Middle East during the Crusades, coupled with a resurgence of classical philosophy, art, and scholarship imported by Byzantine refugees, inspired the Renaissance.

4)
    A.   **Correct.** The peasants and bourgeoisie were dissatisfied with bearing the brunt of the heavy tax burden; meanwhile, poor harvests led to food shortages and panic in rural areas. These factors, along with Enlightenment thought and recent revolutions elsewhere, spurred the French Revolution.

    B.   Incorrect. Napoleon came to power after the French Revolution, providing stability in a chaotic period.

C.   Incorrect. The Congress of Vienna was a conference held after the initial defeat of Napoleon to determine the future of Europe. It occurred after the French Revolution.

D.   Incorrect. The reign of Louis XIV weakened the nobility and centralized power under the king. In the long term, weakening the nobility and isolating them at Versailles contributed to the circumstances that enabled the French Revolution. However, his reign alone did not cause it, and he was long dead by the time the Revolution began.

5)

A.   Incorrect. While the Treaty of Westphalia did end the Thirty Years' War, this answer choice is incomplete given the other possibilities offered.

B.   Incorrect. Again, while this is true, it is incorrect due to the other options presented.

C.   Incorrect. The Treaty of Westphalia is considered the foundation of modern international relations as it is based on the idea of state sovereignty; however, due to the other answer choices, this one is incorrect.

D.   Correct. All of these answer choices are correct.

6)

A.   Incorrect. The Catholic Church was not divided over the Counter-Reformation.

B.   Correct. The Counter-Reformation re-converted Protestants back to Catholicism, spread Catholic education, and fought heresy.

C.   Incorrect. While the Counter-Reformation embraced spreading Catholicism globally, it did not emerge in response to exploration in the Western Hemisphere.

D.   Incorrect. Enlightenment thought did not truly emerge for another century.

8)

A.   Incorrect. Some European powers had already made slavery illegal (legally, if not in practice).

B.   Correct. Abolitionist European powers were unwilling to support the South economically, due to the Confederacy's stance on slavery.

C.   Incorrect. While rapidly industrializing Europe needed cotton, many European countries ceased trade with the states that seceded from the Union and developed sources of cotton elsewhere (in Egypt and India, for example).

D.   Incorrect. B is the correct answer choice.

7)

   A.   Incorrect. France supported the United States in order to weaken the British.

   B.   Incorrect. Spain retained control over its territories in the Americas, which included substantial land in North America.

   C.   **Correct.** The Enlightenment ideals that inspired the American Revolution and the revolution's success helped inspire the French Revolution and other movements.

   D.   Incorrect. International trade continued with the resource-rich United States.

9)

   A.   Incorrect. Oliver Cromwell controlled the country following the Civil War, subduing revolt in Ireland and defeating Charles in Scotland.

   B.   Incorrect. The Glorious Revolution was mainly a religious, not ethnic, movement; in fact, William of Orange was Dutch.

   C.   **Correct.** The Glorious Revolution, in which the Protestants William and Mary deposed the Catholic James II, secured a future of Protestant monarchies in Britain.

   D.   Incorrect. Separatists, not Puritans, wanted to separate from the Church of England; less radical, Puritans sought reform.

10)

   A.   Incorrect. Britain did not occupy China, although it did control Hong Kong, which remained a colony until 1997.

   B.   Incorrect. China was not successful in the Opium Wars.

   C.   Incorrect. Trade treaties at the time did not favor China.

   D.   **Correct.** Britain gained economic and commercial privileges in China it had previously not had, including gaining Hong Kong, freedom of movement in China, and access to ports.

11)

   A.   Incorrect. European control over the Americas was limited by the nineteenth century; furthermore, natural resources gleaned through imperialism went to power industrialization in Europe, not elsewhere.

   B.   **Correct.** The philosophy of taking on the "white man's burden" and the competition for global control of territory between European powers (among other factors) drove imperialism.

   C.   Incorrect. European imperial powers did not fuel industrialization in the Americas.

   D.   Incorrect. European imperialists sought resources to power industry in Europe.

12)

    A.   **Correct.** The valuable routes into and through the Red Sea were essential for the British economy and Britain's connections to its colonies in India, East Africa, South Africa, and Australia. The security of those routes was of paramount importance.

    B.   Incorrect. Mecca and Medina are both inland cities and not major centers of global trade.

    C.   Incorrect. Inland Somalia, with limited natural resources, was not a major concern.

    D.   Incorrect. Britain controlled substantial territory throughout sub-Saharan Africa.

13)

    A.   Incorrect. The 1884 Berlin Conference focused on Africa, not China.

    B.   Incorrect. Spheres of influence were negotiated over time with China and in the context of instability and conflict there, not between European powers alone; furthermore, the Berlin Conference concentrated on imperialism in Africa, not Asia.

    C.   **Correct.** The 1884 Berlin Conference determined the division of Africa into colonies between the European imperial powers. This was done without regard for or consultation with Africans.

    D.   Incorrect. The Triple Alliance was rooted in the collapse of the Three Emperors' League (an alliance between Russia, Germany, and Austria-Hungary); after Germany and Austria-Hungary established the secret Dual Alliance and assisted Italy against France, the Triple Alliance was born. Russia later allied with Britain and France, forming the Triple Entente. These relationships were the basis for the system of alliances leading to the First World War; however, they were not developed at the Berlin Conference.

14)

    A.   **Correct.** The Three Emperors' League reflected the principles of state sovereignty and non-interference.

    B.   Incorrect. The Three Emperors' League was not an active military alliance.

    C.   Incorrect. There was no explicit agreement of financial support in the Three Emperors' League.

    D.   Incorrect. The Three Emperors' League was not a free-trade agreement, nor was it an active military alliance.

15)

A. Incorrect. Russia's strategy was land-based expansion; it did not have a strong navy until the twentieth century.

B. **Correct.** Russia expanded to the east, taking control of Siberia. Russia also extended westward to an extent, controlling part of Eastern Europe.

C. Incorrect. Russia expanded and employed developmental strategies under a number of czars, including Catherine the Great and Peter the Great. In terms of industrialization, some efforts were made under the Romanovs; however, industrialization accelerated under the Soviets.

D. Incorrect. Russia engaged in empire building throughout Eurasia well into the twentieth century; some argue that it has continued to do so in Crimea and Ukraine today.

16)

A. Incorrect. Nationalism did not benefit the Austro-Hungarian Empire: smaller ethnic groups living in territory controlled by the empire wanted their independence due to nationalism.

B. Incorrect. The Austro-Hungarian Empire began losing control over its Balkan territories due to nationalism and due to interference from Russia, which supported Slavic minorities in the Balkans.

C. Incorrect. Nationalism drove ethnic groups to seek self-rule and independence, not representation in government.

D. **Correct.** Nationalism triggered independence movements and advocacy.

17)

A. Incorrect. Many of the boundaries are the modern borders of Middle Eastern countries today, so the region has been greatly affected.

B. **Correct.** Borders did not take into account history or ethnic groups; installed rulers did not necessarily have legitimacy in the eyes of the people, leading to political instability and violence.

C. Incorrect. The protectorates did not improve governance or stabilize the region following the decline of the Ottoman Empire.

D. Incorrect. Outside investment in strategic resources (like oil) has contributed to instability in the region by providing support to illegitimate rulers and contributing to income inequality and conflict.

18)

A. Incorrect. During the Meiji Restoration, Japan abolished traditional institutions like feudalism and began pursuing western-style development.

B. **Correct.** The Meiji Restoration was a period of industrialization and westernization in Japan.

C.   Incorrect. The Meiji Restoration occurred before Japanese imperialism began throughout Asia.

D.   Incorrect. The Meiji Restoration was a socioeconomic movement, not a return to traditional cultural practices.

19)

A.   Incorrect. The American Revolution preceded the French Revolution. Early industrialization had begun in the late eighteenth and early nineteenth centuries, around the same time as the revolutions; however, the First World War would not break out until 1914.

B.   Correct. The American Revolution preceded the French Revolution; resulting instability in France eventually led to the rise of Napoleon. Shifting European alliances triggered the First World War in the early twentieth century.

C.   Incorrect. Like answer choice A, the American Revolution preceded the French Revolution and the Industrial Revolution began at roughly the same time. WWI did not occur until the twentieth century.

D.   Incorrect. The Rape of Nanjing occurred in 1937; otherwise the events are in order.

20)

A.   Incorrect. Italian nationalism inspired unification of the small political entities of the Italian Peninsula.

B.   Correct. The Congress of Vienna followed the Napoleonic Wars; it was a meeting of European powers to determine how to manage Europe.

C.   Incorrect. German unification was largely a result of nationalism, as the small territories of Central Europe united under Prussia thanks to shared language, cultural practices, and other commonalities.

D.   Incorrect. During the Franco-Prussian War, Prussia attacked France to regain control over Alsace-Lorraine, which it had lost to Napoleon. Prussian nationalism, in part, inspired this war, as France was a long-time rival.

21)

A.   Incorrect. These revolutions both opposed the wealthiest elites.

B.   Incorrect. Both revolutions took advantage of the discontented and numerous agricultural workers, but the French bourgeoisie was mainly concerned with limiting its overwhelming tax burden and controlling more land; likewise, the Russian revolutionaries focused on organizing urban industrial workers more than the Russian agricultural workers.

C. Incorrect. This was a socialist ideal, not a goal of the French Revolution.

D. **Correct.** While the peasantry revolted in the countryside and the people stormed the Bastille in 1789, the French Revolution was based on the Enlightenment ideals embodied in the *Declaration of the Rights of Man and Citizen* issued by the National Constituent Assembly dominated by the Bourgeoisie of the Third Estate. Likewise, the Russian Revolution was instigated by Lenin and Trotsky, urban intellectuals inspired by the socialism of Karl Marx. Lenin and Trotsky helped organize the proletariat in a communist revolution overthrowing the tsar.

22)

A. Incorrect. This explanation is insufficient.

B. **Correct.** The main factors in post-WWI German economic collapse are all addressed here.

C. Incorrect. This explanation does not account for global economic depression.

D. Incorrect. This is untrue.

23)

A. Incorrect. China was not a US ally.

B. Incorrect. The Soviet Union was certainly not a US ally.

C. Incorrect. While the People's Republic of China was not represented at the UN, this was not the reason for the Sino-Soviet Split; the USSR recognized the PRC.

D. **Correct.** The Soviet establishment became increasingly alarmed at Maoist interpretations of communism, which differed from Marxism-Leninism.

24)

A. Incorrect. Some scholars date the beginning of WWII to Japan's invasion of Manchuria, which occurred before the 1937 Rape of Nanjing.

B. Incorrect. Japan annexed Korea in 1910 following the growth of its influence in East Asia after the Russo-Japanese War and other developments. This was before the First World War.

C. **Correct.** Given Japan's role as an Axis power and the conflict in East Asia, some historians believe that WWII began with Japan's invasion of Manchuria in 1931, earlier than Hitler's invasion of Poland in 1939.

D. Incorrect. The Chinese Civil War took place throughout the 1930s and after WWII; it was not a cause of the Second World War.

25)

A. Incorrect. While decolonization resulted in independence for former colonies (usually following a period of international or United Nations supervision), this answer choice is incorrect given the other options presented.

B. Incorrect. The United Nations took a leading role in decolonization; however, this answer choice is incomplete.

C. Incorrect. Some countries experienced lengthy and brutal conflict in fighting for their independence and periods of violent instability after independence; again, though, this is not a complete answer given the other choices.

D. Correct. All of the answer choices provided are true.

26)

A. Incorrect. Afghanistan did not come under Indian influence, although it did become vulnerable to extremist influences.

B. Correct. Afghanistan became unstable and entered into a period of civil war that ended only with the rise of the extremist Taliban, who brought stability to much of the country—along with an ideology embracing tribalism and extremely traditional Islamic values.

C. Incorrect. While greatly influenced by Pakistan, Afghanistan did not join that country.

D. Incorrect. Technically, neither NATO nor any other international organization governed Afghanistan, though a US-led international presence strongly influenced Afghan politics during the United States' war in Afghanistan in the early twenty-first century.

27)

A. Correct. The Warsaw Pact was a mutual defense agreement between Eastern European countries and the USSR in response to NATO.

B. Incorrect. The Warsaw Pact included more than two countries.

C. Incorrect. While it could be argued that the Warsaw Pact reflected Soviet control over Eastern Europe, this answer choice is not specific enough.

D. Incorrect. The Warsaw Pact was defense agreement, not simply a political division.

28)

A. Correct. Only nine years after independence, Somalia endured a coup and came under a dictatorship. A strong civil society would have strengthened a democratic government, making it less susceptible to a coup.

B. Incorrect. Somalia's alliance with the USSR was clearly strategic as it attacked a Soviet ally and willingly accepted aid from the United States.

C. Incorrect. Somalia was clearly divided among clans, leading to Barre's downfall.

D. Incorrect. Improving ties with the communist Soviet Union would not improve a country's position in the global capitalist market; furthermore, under Barre, conflict and shifting allegiances, not international trade, were priorities.

29)

A. Incorrect. While this is true, it is not typical of most former colonies in Africa.

B. Correct. The boundaries of many African countries were created at the 1885 Berlin Conference when Africa was divided among European powers; as a result, ethnic groups have been separated by international borders and many countries have a limited or no sense of national identity.

C. Incorrect. Somalia experimented with alliances with both Cold War powers.

D. Incorrect. The United Nations provided a forum where many small countries—former African colonies among them—could develop diplomatic blocs (such as the Non-Aligned Movement) and effectively increase their influence in international affairs.

30)

A. Incorrect. As the conflict was a proxy war between the Cold War powers, the United States and Soviet Union never came into military conflict.

B. Incorrect. The US and USSR did not seek a diplomatic solution to resolve the conflict.

C. Correct. The Cold War powers did not take direct military action in the war between Somalia and Ethiopia.

D. Incorrect. As a proxy war between the US and USSR, the conflict was a Cold War phenomenon.

US History to 1877

1)

A. Incorrect. The Mayflower Compact was written by one Christian group—Separatists.

B. Incorrect. The Mayflower Compact articulated terms of governance among European settlers; it was not a treaty with other parties.

C. **Correct.** As a governing document, the Mayflower Compact was notable in that it provided for governance with the consent of the governed, a departure from British rule.

D. Incorrect. The Mayflower Compact was written by Separatists.

2)

A. **Correct.** Southern geography and climate lent itself to labor-intensive plantation agriculture, for which the colonists exploited slave labor. Natural harbors in the north fostered urban development, while the land was more appropriate for smaller farms.

B. Incorrect. The reverse was true.

C. Incorrect. All the colonies had wealthy, elite classes, in addition to working classes, indentured servants, and slaves.

D. Incorrect. Economic and cultural differences developed among the colonies.

3)

A. Incorrect. While some colonists were quite wealthy, colonial wealth paled in the face of British wealth.

B. Incorrect. The colonists did not have superior weaponry.

C. **Correct.** The colonial military did have strong leaders, and an intimate knowledge of the terrain, many having been born there.

D. Incorrect. Britain had an experienced military with substantial experience fighting in Europe and elsewhere. In addition, King George III hired Hessian mercenaries from Germany to supplement British troops.

4)

A. Incorrect. While tobacco was a major source of income for the British, this answer choice does not sufficiently respond to the question.

B. Incorrect. Rice was an important crop in the mid-Atlantic colonies; however, this response is incomplete given the other answer choices.

C.   Incorrect. While beaver pelts were essential to North American trade, particularly throughout Canada, this answer choice is incomplete.

D.   Correct. Tobacco, rice, and beaver pelts were all enormously popular in Europe and very profitable North American resources.

5)

A.   Incorrect. The British and French colonial presence did not extend as far west as the Sioux and Cheyenne lands.

B.   Correct. During the French and Indian War, the British were allied with the Iroquois and the French with the Algonquin throughout the northeast (today, Ontario, Upstate New York, and the Great Lakes region).

C.   Incorrect. The Cherokee and Seminole were not involved in British-French conflict.

D.   Incorrect. Colonial power did not reach as far west as Apache territory.

6)

A.   Incorrect. The views of the Federalists and Anti-Federalists differed a great deal.

B.   Incorrect. The Bill of Rights was a compromise measure; it was not originally a Federalist contribution.

C.   Incorrect. The reverse was true.

D.   Correct. The Federalists were the driving force behind a stronger Constitution that would empower the United States federal government; the Anti-Federalists worked to protect state sovereignty and ensured the passage of the Bill of Rights to protect certain rights not explicitly guaranteed in the Constitution itself.

7)

A.   Correct. The Democratic-Republicans, descended from the Anti-Federalists, opposed a strong federal government and urban business interests, focusing on agrarian issues.

B.   Incorrect. The Democratic-Republicans focused on rural constituents.

C.   Incorrect. While the Democratic-Republicans surely did not favor a strong federal government, their priority was not supporting big business or banking.

D.   Incorrect. The Democratic-Republicans were against federalism.

8)

A. Incorrect. This did not occur until after Jackson had been elected president.

B. **Correct.** Jackson was extremely popular among the lower classes and rural farmers of the South; changing voting laws to allow dispossessed white males to vote expanded the electorate, giving him a huge advantage.

C. Incorrect. Jackson was unpopular with the elite landowners of the North.

D. Incorrect. Jackson and Calhoun were fierce rivals with a poor personal and professional relationship.

9)

A. **Correct.** Hispanic residents of the land the United States gained in the Treaty of Guadalupe Hidalgo did not obtain all they were promised; in fact, many lost their property and were not treated equally under the law or in society.

B. Incorrect. Those Hispanic residents of Mexico who were living on territory ceded to the United States did not receive restitution for losses suffered in violation of the Treaty of Guadalupe Hidalgo.

C. Incorrect. Latinos and Latinas living in United States territory often experienced unequal treatment under the law and in social situations.

D. Incorrect. Many people of Mexican descent stayed in what became the United States following the Mexican-American War.

10)

A. Incorrect. An individual president was not limited to two terms of service until the twentieth century.

B. Incorrect. The system of checks and balances, as built into the Constitution, includes the judicial branch.

C. Incorrect. While civilian oversight of the military is an important part of the American government, this answer choice does not properly describe the system of checks and balances reinforced by the three branches of government.

D. **Correct.** The Constitutional system of checks and balances is comprised of the three branches of government, which limit each other, thereby limiting federal power.

11)

A. **Correct.** Adams was a staunch Federalist who arguably veered into federal overreach with the Alien and Sedition Acts during his presidency.

B. Incorrect. As a Federalist, Adams believed the opposite.

C. Incorrect. The Bill of Rights was a concession to Anti-Federalists, who feared the Constitution did not adequately protect states' and individual rights.

D. Incorrect. The Constitutional Convention was called upon recognition that the Articles of Confederation were too weak.

12)

A.   Incorrect. The Industrial Revolution began in Britain when new technology allowed the faster and more organized production of goods.

B.   Correct. The Second Great Awakening was characterized by religious movements like utopianism; interest in romanticism in the arts and humanism led to abolitionism and early progressive ideals.

C.   Incorrect. The Enlightenment was a seventeenth- and eighteenth-century phenomenon in Europe.

D.   Incorrect. The Glorious Revolution had taken place in England over a century before.

13)

A.   Incorrect. The Monroe Doctrine did not attempt to assert US power beyond the Western Hemisphere.

B.   Incorrect. The Monroe Doctrine encompassed Latin America, not just the United States.

C.   Correct. The Monroe Doctrine was a US policy designed to insulate Latin America from European influence, increasing US dominance in the region.

D.   Incorrect. While the Monroe Doctrine did result in increased US international involvement, this choice does not specifically answer the question.

14)

A.   Incorrect. France and the early United States had a complex relationship, but this was not the central reason for US anxiety over the Louisiana Purchase.

B.   Correct. Despite Jefferson's position as an Anti-Federalist Democrat, he had used executive powers as president to negotiate the purchase without congressional consultation, considered by many as federal overreach.

C.   Incorrect. The needs of Native Americans were not a pressing issue for most Americans, as they considered strategic control of land and, eventually, westward expansion, to be necessary.

D.   Incorrect. This was not the most pressing concern for most Americans, who were still preoccupied with preventing a dictatorship.

15)

A.   Incorrect. At the time, slavery was legal throughout the United States.

B.   Incorrect. Three-quarters of the states must ratify amendments in order for them to take effect.

C.   Correct. The Three-Fifths Compromise accounted for slaves as part of a state's population (although they could not vote or enjoy the same rights as white citizens).

D.   Incorrect. Nine states needed to ratify the Constitution for it to go into effect.

16)

A.   Incorrect. The Louisiana Purchase did not include Texas.

B.   Incorrect. The territory did not extend to the Pacific Ocean.

C.   Incorrect. While Lewis and Clark explored this area, the Louisiana Purchase did not include territory through Oregon—control over this land was disputed by the British.

D.   Correct. The United States gained the valuable Port of New Orleans and Mississippi River.

17)

A.   Incorrect. Today, Constitutionalists refers to politicians and members of the judiciary who believe in following the Constitution today exactly as it was written; it was not a term used in the late eighteenth century.

B.   Incorrect. The Revolution was over by the time of the Constitutional Convention.

C.   Incorrect. Federalists were content with the Constitution as it was written.

D.   Correct. Anti-Federalists would not accept the Constitution without the Bill of Rights, believing it did not go far enough to protect individual and states' rights.

18)

A.   Incorrect. The War of 1812 is widely considered to have ended in a stalemate.

B.   Correct. Tecumseh and the Confederacy wanted to halt US expansion and maintain control over their land.

C.   Incorrect. Tecumseh never allied with the US.

D.   Incorrect. The British army did not collapse.

19)

A.   Incorrect. The Fugitive Slave Act allowed slave owners, not states, to pursue escaped slaves.

B.   Correct. The Fugitive Slave Act—a federal law—actually benefitted those states' rights advocates who also favored slavery.

C.   Incorrect. The Fugitive Slave Act did not allow states to carry out police actions.

D.   Incorrect. The Fugitive Slave Act applied to individuals, not states.

20)

A.   Incorrect. The South's technological resources were inferior to those of the North.

B.   Incorrect. European countries ceased trade with the South, finding alternative sources of cotton in protest of slavery.

C.   Correct. The Confederacy had excellent military leaders; many Confederate leaders and much of the population strongly believed in the right of states to make decisions without federal interference, not only about slavery but also about trade and other issues.

D.   Incorrect. The Confederacy had limited infrastructure.

21)

A.   Incorrect. The Supreme Court ruled against Dred Scott, who was an escaped slave.

B.   Correct. The ruling reinforced the Fugitive Slave Act by forcing Scott to return to a life of slavery.

C.   Incorrect. The ruling strengthened not only the Fugitive Slave Act, but also the Kansas-Nebraska Act; thus, it effectively abolished the Missouri Compromise.

D.   Incorrect. The court did not abolish the Fugitive Slave Act.

22)

A.   Incorrect. While slavery and states' rights to allow it were essential elements of these pieces of legislation, this answer is incomplete in the context of the other choices.

B.   Incorrect. Indeed, the compromises were reached in order to resolve disagreements among politicians; however, this answer is not sufficient, given the other answer choices.

C.   Incorrect. The United States was deeply divided over the role of the federal government, and this division manifested through slavery; still, this answer choice is incorrect given the other choices available.

D.   Correct. All of the answer choices are true.

23)

A.   Incorrect. African Americans could not vote until the Fifteenth Amendment was ratified.

B.   Incorrect. Native Americans did not have a political voice in the US.

C.   Incorrect. Popular sovereignty would still benefit settlers in the territories in the long term by increasing their political power.

D.   Correct. Popular sovereignty made the expansion of slavery possible.

24)

A.   Incorrect. The Dred Scott decision upheld the Fugitive Slave Act.

B.   Incorrect. The Compromise of 1850 only permitted the possibility of slavery in a small section of land north of the thirty-sixth parallel in the far West (parts of Utah).

C.   Correct. The Kansas-Nebraska Act allowed slavery north of the thirty-sixth parallel throughout the Plains and the Western territories which the Missouri Compromise had previously forbidden.

D.   Incorrect. The Fugitive Slave Act did not determine where slavery was legal.

25)

A.   Correct. By blocking the South's access to strategic waterways, the Union was able to prevent cotton exports and other vital trade, "strangling" the Confederacy economically.

B.   Incorrect. The South was primarily a rural economy.

C.   Incorrect. The Anaconda Plan envisioned surrounding the entire South, not just Richmond.

D.   Incorrect. The Anaconda Plan strategically interrupted trade; it did not take a tactical military approach.

26)

A.   Incorrect. The Federalist Party had declined in the early nineteenth century and never returned to the political scene.

B.   Correct. The Civil War devastated the South's economy due to infrastructural damage and international isolation.

C.   Incorrect. The Republican Party appeared before the Civil War.

D.   Incorrect. The Southern economy suffered from the Civil War.

27)

A.   Incorrect. Conditions for most freed slaves did not immediately improve; they continued to face widespread violence and discrimination.

B.   Incorrect. With damage to agricultural land and existing infrastructure, the Southern economy and many Southerners suffered; Reconstruction programs did not immediately take effect.

C.   Incorrect. Radical Republicans felt that the Reconstruction Acts did not go far enough in punishing the South; others in Congress felt they were too harsh. Likewise, many in the South felt they were unfair.

D.   Correct. The Reconstruction Acts effectively placed the South under martial law.

28)

    A.   Incorrect. The Fifteenth Amendment only enabled African American men to vote. No American women could vote in national elections until the ratification of the Nineteenth Amendment in 1920.

    B.   Incorrect. African American women were still unable to vote, even though the Fifteenth Amendment allowed African American men to exercise that right. African American women would not be able to vote until 1920.

    C.   Incorrect. The Fourteenth Amendment ensures equal protection under the law to all Americans, regardless of race, gender, or other categories.

    D.   **Correct.** The Thirteenth Amendment abolished slavery; the Fourteenth Amendment promised equal protection under the law to all US citizens; the Fifteenth Amendment ensured that (male) African Americans and former slaves could vote.

29)

    A.   **Correct.** Sharecropping perpetuated racial inequality in the South.

    B.   Incorrect. The Colored Farmers' Alliance assisted African American farmers.

    C.   Incorrect. The Reconstruction Acts did not include this provision.

    D.   Incorrect. While labor unions championed urban workers, most of whom were white, this was not in direct opposition to efforts to advance African Americans in the South; indeed, the Progressive movement brought together activists for these and many diverse causes.

30)

    A.   Incorrect. Assimilation destroyed many people's connection with their cultures and traditions, but this answer choice is incomplete in the context of the other options.

    B.   Incorrect. Again, forcing children to leave their families for white schools destroyed their connection with their languages, cultures, and traditions. Moreover, these actions injured their personal bonds with their families and communities—further weakening tribal societies. However, this answer choice is insufficient, given the other answer choices available.

    C.   Incorrect. Forcing people to leave their homelands for assigned living spaces on reservations fostered social breakdown by interrupting traditional connections with land and dispossessing people of their homes. Again, however, this answer choice is incomplete.

    D.   **Correct.** All of the above are true.

US History 1877 – Present

1)

A. **Correct.** The United States was the aggressor in the Spanish-American War—it was never definitively proven that the *Maine* was actually attacked by Spain. Furthermore, the war was fought in several different theaters worldwide.

B. Incorrect. The First World War took place after all of these conflicts.

C. Incorrect. The Texan Revolution occurred before Texas joined the United States.

D. Incorrect. The War of 1812 was partially due to British provocations and took place entirely on US and British Canadian soil.

2)

A. Incorrect. The Senate never ratified the Treaty of Versailles, so the United States never joined the League of Nations.

B. Incorrect. NATO formed after WWII.

C. Incorrect. The United States did not ratify the Treaty of Versailles.

D. **Correct.** None of the above are true.

3)

A. Incorrect. While many businessmen had become extremely wealthy due to trusts, antitrust legislation was not explicitly designed to reduce wealth altogether.

B. Incorrect. Antitrust legislation was intended to create a fairer marketplace, not redistribute existing wealth.

C. **Correct.** Trusts had monopolized the marketplace; thus the market required intervention.

D. Incorrect. While trusts, having monopolized the markets, could effectively control prices, this was not the explicit reason for antitrust legislation.

4)

A. Incorrect. Temperance activists believed alcohol was harmful to society.

B. Incorrect. Temperance activists were unconcerned with alcohol prices, believing that it destroyed families and thus should not be consumed at all.

C. **Correct.** Temperance activists feared the negative impact of alcohol on poor and working class families.

D. Incorrect. The United States was a major producer of alcohol.

5)

A.   Incorrect. The Seneca Falls Convention called for women's suffrage; however, women would not be able to vote for another seventy-two years.

B.   Correct. The Nineteenth Amendment allowed women to vote; it was ratified in 1920.

C.   Incorrect. The Equal Rights Amendment was never ratified.

D.   Incorrect. The Voting Rights Act of 1965 protected the voting rights of African Americans.

6)

A.   Incorrect. Labor unions formed to address unfair wages (or non-payment of them altogether).

B.   Incorrect. Overwork was an important issue addressed by labor unions.

C.   Correct. Labor unions sought improved working conditions, not the overthrow of capitalism.

D.   Incorrect. Workers used labor unions to protest dangerous working conditions.

7)

A.   Incorrect. Social Darwinism is not related to the theory of evolution.

B.   Correct. Social Darwinism was the idea that the wealthiest and more privileged (generally, white people) deserved their power because they were inherently stronger than and more fit for survival and success than poorer people and those of other races.

C.   Incorrect. Again, Social Darwinism was unrelated to evolution.

D.   Incorrect. Social Darwinism was applied to humans and social groups, not the animal kingdom.

8)

A.   Incorrect. Castro was already in power at the time of the Cuban Missile Crisis.

B.   Incorrect. Fidel Castro has remained in power, at least in name, through 2015; his brother Raul controls Cuba, and despite many reforms, the same government is in place.

C.   Correct. Following the extreme tensions between the two countries, the United States and the Soviet Union improved dialogue in the early 1960s, leading to a period of détente.

D.   Incorrect. The Cuban Missile Crisis led to a period of détente; it did not end one.

9)

A.   Incorrect. SALT and SALT II were arms agreements, so the two countries were engaged in diplomatic discourse.

B.   Incorrect. Given that these agreements led to limitations of strategic arms for both countries, they were not indicative of active conflict.

C.   Incorrect. Glasnost was a policy of openness in the Soviet Union under Gorbachev.

D.   Correct. SALT and SALT II were reached during periods of diplomatic détente when productive dialogue between the Cold War powers was possible.

10)

A.   Correct. Roosevelt actually used the Interstate Commerce Act to carry out its original purpose: to break up trusts. By prosecuting the powerful Northern Securities railroad company, he became known as a "trust buster."

B.   Incorrect. FDR developed the Works Progress Administration as part of the New Deal.

C.   Incorrect. The Sixteenth Amendment was ratified after Theodore Roosevelt's presidency.

D.   Incorrect. Roosevelt implemented antitrust acts widely.

11)

A.   Correct. Public paranoia over communism was widespread, and many public figures were accused of being communist.

B.   Incorrect. The United States never supported Maoism.

C.   Incorrect. No members of Congress were removed from office due to the McCarthy hearings.

D.   Incorrect. No members of Congress were revealed to be Soviet spies during the McCarthy hearings.

12)

A.   Incorrect. The Iranian Revolution established a theocratic government that would become radically anti-American; the hostage crisis was led by activist students.

B.   Correct. President Carter's inability to resolve the crisis helped propel Ronald Reagan to victory in the 1980 presidential election; Reagan took an aggressive stance against the Soviet Union and escalated the arms race, intensifying the Cold War throughout the 1980s.

C.   Incorrect. The Soviet Union's invasion of Afghanistan was unrelated to the Iranian hostage crisis, even though it did occur in the same year.

D.   Incorrect. President Carter lost the election, in part due to ineffective negotiations with Iran; furthermore, the 1980s were a tense period between the United States and the Soviet Union.

13)

A.   Incorrect. The US government did not even acknowledge wrongdoing for another forty years.

B.   Incorrect. In *Korematsu v. US*, the legality of internment came before the Supreme Court; however, it was upheld.

C.   Correct. Japanese-Americans were dispossessed and unfairly treated as potential traitors, even though they had lived in the United States for generations.

D.   Incorrect. Most camps were located on the West Coast.

14)

A.   Incorrect. OPEC did place an embargo on the US for supporting Israel. However, even though OPEC is comprised of many Middle Eastern countries, the Middle East did not suffer economically as much as the United States did because it supplies oil to countries worldwide.

B.   Correct. In retaliation for its support for Israel, OPEC placed an oil embargo on the United States. OPEC's embargo strongly harmed the US economy, which was very dependent on Middle Eastern oil at the time.

C.   Incorrect. Arab support for the United States decreased due to its support for Israel.

D.   Incorrect. The United States' relationships with Saudi Arabia and Iran were strained by its support for Israel.

15)

A.   Correct. Head Start was introduced to provide early childhood support for low-income families; the Department of Housing and Urban Development became a cabinet-level agency in 1965.

B.   Incorrect. Social Security was created as part of the New Deal.

C.   Incorrect. Social Security already existed when Johnson became president.

D.   Incorrect. While Head Start and the Department of Housing and Urban Development were initiatives connected to the War on Poverty, Social Security was not.

16)

A.   Incorrect. Cesar Chavez and the UFW organized Mexican and Mexican-American workers already present in the United States. They focused on the rights of workers in the US

B.   Correct. Cesar Chavez and the UFW advocated for the rights of Mexican and Mexican-American farmworkers in the US, who were often disadvantaged; moreover, the activism of the UFW set a precedent for later advocacy in support of Hispanic Americans.

C.   Incorrect. Cesar Chavez and the UFW were mainly active in California and the Southwest, not Texas.

D.   Incorrect. B is the correct answer.

17)

A.   Incorrect. Gay Pride rallies and marches were not major features of the public landscape until after the Stonewall Riots.

B.   Incorrect. Milk's election was an important development in LGBT rights as openly gay public figures were rare, but his election occurred after the Stonewall Riots.

C.   Incorrect. Again, the public discourse and activism that resulted from the AIDS crisis helped bring LGBT issues into the mainstream public sphere, but these events happened in the 1980s and 1990s.

D.   Correct. Generally viewed as the beginning of the LGBT rights movement, the Stonewall Riots occurred in response to ongoing police harassment of the gay community in New York City and resulted in a more organized push for civil rights.

18)

A.   Incorrect. Each believed the opposite.

B.   Correct. Dr. King focused on integration, while Malcolm X focused on black empowerment.

C.   Incorrect. Both believed in social change.

D.   Incorrect. On some issues, they took very different positions.

19)

A.   Incorrect. President Nixon resigned.

B.   Incorrect. Watergate unfolded during Nixon's second term.

C.   Correct. Watergate destroyed many Americans' trust in the government, which had already been weakened after the turbulent 1960s and the Vietnam War.

D.   Incorrect. Watergate did not change the two-party system.

20)

    A.   Incorrect. Conservatives believe in free trade, but not in open borders and unrestricted movement of people.

    B.   **Correct.** Conservatives believe in low taxes to boost business.

    C.   Incorrect. Conservatives believe in minimal interference with businesses and the marketplace.

    D.   Incorrect. Conservatives would likely support efficiency in the military, but believe in a large and strong one.

21)

    A.   Incorrect. While the Taliban harbored Osama bin Laden, they themselves had not directly attacked the United States and were not the primary reason for the US invasion.

    B.   **Correct.** Neutralizing Osama bin Laden and his network—al Qaeda—was the stated objective for the invasion of Afghanistan.

    C.   Incorrect. Al Qaeda was not the government of Afghanistan.

    D.   Incorrect. Al Qaeda was not believed to have weapons of mass destruction in Afghanistan.

22)

    A.   Incorrect. The Patriot Act was created before the invasion of Iraq.

    B.   Incorrect. The Patriot Act affected the US domestically.

    C.   Incorrect. The Patriot Act did not establish the detention centers at Guantanamo Bay.

    D.   **Correct.** The Patriot Act gave the federal government unprecedented surveillance powers over Americans within the United States.

23)

    A.   Incorrect. Concerns over privacy were related to the Patriot Act; no known surveillance programs were based in Guantanamo.

    B.   Incorrect. Many lawmakers argued vehemently against transferring prisoners to facilities on US soil.

    C.   **Correct.** Lack of clarity over the status of prisoners at Guantanamo Bay and their treatment was—and remains—controversial.

    D.   Incorrect. This is not known to be the case.

Go on →

24)

    A.   **Correct.** The invasion and occupation of Iraq was part of the War on Terror and in accordance with President Bush's doctrine of preemption—that the US should preempt terrorist attacks by attacking threats first. Erroneous beliefs that Saddam Hussein had weapons of mass destruction and was linked to al Qaeda were reasons for the invasion.

    B.   Incorrect. Osama bin Laden was not believed to be in Iraq; some argued that he was linked with Saddam Hussein, but there was very little evidence of such an alliance as the two had divergent ideologies.

    C.   Incorrect. No partnership between Iraq and al Qaeda was ever uncovered; furthermore, al Qaeda did not use any weapons on 9/11 to attack the United States (aside from box cutters to threaten the airline pilots)—it hijacked airplanes and crashed them into buildings.

    D.   Incorrect. Iraq had nothing to do with the terrorist attacks on the United States on September 11, 2001.

25)

    A.   Incorrect. The Reagan administration focused on the arms race, not diplomatic engagement.

    B.   Incorrect. Under Reagan, the US fought proxy wars in Central America, Afghanistan, and elsewhere, but did not directly confront the USSR militarily.

    C.   Incorrect. Multilateral diplomacy was not a US priority at this time.

    D.   **Correct.** The Reagan administration focused on arms buildup, weapons spending, and supporting anti-Soviet movements around the world.

26)

    A.   Incorrect. While Truman certainly suggests that one way of life is better than the other, his description is more complicated.

    B.   Incorrect. He describes one way of life as free from political oppression with personal freedoms; he describes the other as politically and socially limited.

    C.   Incorrect. Truman paints a picture of starkly different societies, one with political freedoms and the other without.

    D.   **Correct.** Truman described two ways of life: one politically and socially repressive, the other politically and socially free.

27)

    A.   Incorrect. While this is the general idea, Truman expresses more specific policy objectives.

    B.   Incorrect. Truman is alluding to international security, not sovereignty.

    C.   **Correct.** Truman suggests that totalitarianism threatens US security; hence, it must be prevented.

    D.   Incorrect. Truman offers a more aggressive stance here.

28)

    A.   **Correct.** Truman is contrasting the democratic, capitalist United States and the communist Soviet Union.

    B.   Incorrect. The European Union did not yet exist.

    C.   Incorrect. Nazi Germany no longer existed.

    D.   Incorrect. The Soviet Union was a communist, not a fascist, country.

29)

    A.   Incorrect. Hitler's occupation of these territories took place years before Truman's speech.

    B.   **Correct.** Truman presents the Soviet threat here, not the Nazi threat, which was already eliminated in the Second World War.

    C.   Incorrect. The Berlin Wall was not built until 1961.

    D.   Incorrect. The Iron Curtain was a figurative description, not a literal construction.

30)

    A.   **Correct.** Truman laid out the Truman Doctrine—containment of communism—in this speech.

    B.   Incorrect. Truman discusses two ways of life, but goes farther and places judgement upon them.

    C.   Incorrect. This is not the main point of the speech.

    D.   Incorrect. Again, this is not the main point of the speech.

Follow the link below to take your second Praxis World and US History (5941) practice test and to access other online study resources:

www.cirrustestprep.com/praxis-5941-online-resources

Made in the USA
Monee, IL
02 March 2025

13277580R00103